INVEST LIKE
WARREN BUFFETT,
LIVE LIKE
JIMMY BUFFETT

INVEST LIKE WARREN BUFFETT, LIVE LIKE JIMMY BUFFETT

A Money Manual for Those
Who Haven't Won the Lottery

LUKI VAIL, CFP

A Birch Lane Press Book
Published by Carol Publishing Group

A Birch Lane Press Book
Published by Carol Publishing Group
Birch Lane Press is a registered trademark of Carol Communications, Inc.

Editorial, sales and distribution, rights and permissions inquiries should be addressed to Carol Publishing Group, 120 Enterprise Avenue, Secaucus, N.J. 07094

In Canada: Canadian Manda Group, One Atlantic Avenue, Suite 105, Toronto, Ontario M6K 3E7

Carol Publishing Group books may be purchased in bulk at special discounts for sales promotion, fund-raising, or educational purposes. Special editions can be created to specifications. For details, contact: Special Sales Department, 120 Enterprise Avenue, Secaucus, N.J. 07094

Manufactured in the United States of America
10 9 8 7 6 5 4 3 2 1

Library of Congress Cataloging-in-Publication Data
Vail, Luki, 1937–
    Invest like Warren Buffett, live like Jimmy Buffett : a money manual for those who haven't won the lottery / Luki Vail.
        p.   cm.
    "A Birch Lane Press book."
    ISBN 1-55972-372-6 (hc)
    1. Finance, Personal.   2. Investments.   3. Retirement—Planning.   I. Title.
    HG179.V317   1996
    332.024—dc20   96-28949
                                                              CIP

Although the author has extensively researched all sources to ensure the accuracy and completeness of the information contained in this book, all content is to be viewed as general information only and should not be construed as actual legal, accounting or financial advice of a personal nature. The ideas, suggestions, general principles, and conclusions presented in this book are subject to local, state, and federal laws and regulations. The continual changing economic, political, and international environment could possibly demand reinterpretation of some or all of the concepts presented herein. Readers should consult a financial expert for specific applications to their individual situations.

Contents

Contents

Contents   xi

Acknowledgments

To my mom, Lucia Styskal. My mother has been invested in the stock market since she married my dad back in 1933. Today, at eighty-three years of age, 98 percent of her money is invested in the stock market. From these years of experience she will tell you, "A dip in the stock market is merely a paper loss. Don't sell. Stay the course. It always comes back."

To Steven Schragis at Carol Publishing for making this book possible. To attorney Judith Copeland from San Diego; accountant Don Perkins; Jim Houle, CPA from Tustin, California; Michael Silverberg, CFP from Lake Forest, California; Jim Sears at Resources Trust Company in Denver, Colorado; and attorney Tom Styskal from Tustin, California, for their technical support.

To Marilyn Burnett for editing this book, and Bob Haxton for guiding me during my first efforts to organize this book. To my friend, Jerry Fagersten, for being available for the myriad of details that came up while putting the finishing touches on the book.

And, last but not least, to my clients, students, friends, and family for their constant encouragement.

Foreword

About This Book and You

Do you ever compare yourself to a mastodon stuck in a prehistoric tar pit when you think about your finances? Trying to relieve your guilt, you trot down to the local bookstore, select the most appealing book, and lug it home. With every intention of absorbing this newfound fountain of knowledge, you sit down that evening with the determination of an astronaut to conquer the unknown.

If you don't fall asleep after reading twenty pages, you realize it was written for the stereotypical family in *Life With Father.* It missed the point about your life. Twenty minutes later you reach instinctively for the TV remote control, and you hate sitcoms.

While researching and writing this book one fact presented itself over and over: Virtually every book about money management written previously was written for your father and his father. As authors Ken Dychtwald and Joe Flower of the futuristic book *Age Wave* point out, "Until recently American lives had been very neat and predictable. We learned, worked, and retired at age sixty-five, and shortly thereafter died.

"In earlier generations, by the time you were fifty, the kids had graduated from college, the mortgage was paid, and the dog had died. Today, our lives boast nowhere near that level of certainty." The simple fact is we're all living longer. You can look forward to not only a longer life but a healthier longer life. Because of this, you're redefining "middle" and "old" age.

While pondering this gain, you face financial pressures which include the monumental costs of your children's college years, your aging parents living longer, medical costs rising while benefits are being reduced, and a faltering Social Security system that "probably won't be there for us," alleges Karen Meredith, thirty-nine, a Dallas-area Certified Public Accountant and founder of the American Association of Boomers. Many people's lives have been disrupted by divorce, while others face a dwindling number of job promotions, and others face terminations because of the downsizing of corporations due to the corporations' changes in direction, priorities, or ownership. As part of this four-wheel-drive generation, concerns and questions reel through your head:

"Do we make enough money to support our current lifestyle?"

"How can I possibly retire and have the same quality of life that my parents enjoyed?"

"Where did all those ideals and fantasies of yesterday go?"

"Where does all our money go?"

"My life is that of a fireman, fighting fires and serving mundane routines."

Financial success does not originate from formulas and techniques. It begins with knowing yourself well: what you love to do and what your incentives are. This book will help you establish your financial objectives and supply the strategies that will enable you to accomplish them.

In the first section, entitled Treadmills and Visions, you discover how antiquated social influences have subtly influenced your life to this point; what the financial impact of a longer life span means to you; and four ways to master career strategies for job safety.

In the second section, entitled Off the Treadmill in Four Workouts, you learn how to identify what is most important to you; your hidden values that control your incentives; and what money means to you.

In the third section, entitled Jump-Start the Quality of Your Life, you grasp how to clean up your finances in thirteen weeks; and adapt your spending habits to support your goals by understanding how to identify what costs you money, accumulate money effortlessly, position your money to work harder for you, and compile your taxes faster and easier.

In the fourth section, entitled What Costs You Money, you investigate how you can make better use of your money. You learn eight honest tax-fighting tactics; eleven questions to ask about your company's retirement plan; twenty-six ways to cut your insurance bill, yet maximize your family's protection; strategies to increase your college-age child's chances for financial aid; how to deal with the financial and psychological concerns of your aging parents; and how to determine when and why a trust should be made.

In the fifth section, entitled What Makes You Money, you master how to make inflation work for you; employ eight simple rules when choosing a mutual fund; and get answers to three questions to ask a broker.

In the sixth section, entitled The Years Beyond 2011, you ascertain how to weigh occurring economic and social changes today for tomorrow's financial independence; establish strategies for long-term investments to make today for your later years; and, finally, evaluate trends and demographics providing you with control over your financial future.

There are relatively few common-sense things you need to know about money. *Invest Like Warren Buffett, Live like Jimmy Buffett* provides the fundamentals for you to unfold your own hidden incentives and generate your own financial awareness. To get you off to a quick start, pick out one or two concepts a month and make them a part of your life. The next month, add two more strategies. This way you won't become overwhelmed with concepts and strategies. Instead, they will become a way of life for you and your subconscious. Your new awareness will automatically direct your decisions to produce financially favorable results for you and yours.

I

Treadmills and Visions

1

A Different Generation

Few people think more than two or three times a year; I have made an international reputation for myself by thinking once or twice a week.

—George Bernard Shaw

The leading edge of the boomer generation, the one that coined the phrase, "Never trust anyone over thirty," has finally reached middle age. Your generation of 76 million Americans is far from predictable or homogeneous. Born in that eighteen-year span between 1946 and 1964, you are not all megabuck materialists as depicted by the 22,000 articles portraying the myth of the "yuppie."

From the time boomers blazoned that proclamation to today, you have been starting families late, changing careers, and facing permanent job uncertainty. "This is the first generation whose careers won't last for a working lifetime," says Peter A. Morrison, a RAND Corp. demographer. "Midlife career redirection has become more commonplace."

Through all this, your generation fueled the fitness revolution, and, when health-aware boomers turn sixty-five, many will still have the constitutions of fit forty-five-year-olds. The catch to this glowing forecast of living longer is you will

3

have to support yourself longer than any generation in the history of civilization.

Reality 2011

With this whole new definition of aging, you have the opportunity to take on new challenges many times in your life. Rather than being limited to just one career, you may want to work for ten or fifteen years and then take a couple of years off for trips with your family, for new learning experiences, or to just stoke the ol' engine.

Bill Watterson, the creator of the "Calvin and Hobbes" cartoon strip, is taking a nine-month leave from his job. "The strip requires a great deal of research, and I need to do more interplanetary exploration and paleontology work before I continue," Watterson told the *Los Angeles Times*. In 1983, Garry Trudeau went on sabbatical and stopped drawing "Doonesbury" to pursue other projects for twenty months.

Creative Mind Shifting

Your financial success is only a part of your overall success and comes from always seeking new challenges. Discovering new challenges is the result of taking the time to look at your anxieties, interests, and problems from different angles, similar to the way a professional photographer takes rolls and rolls of pictures when shooting an important subject. She'll change the angle, the lighting, and the focus with each shot in order to get the one picture she'll love the most.

To change the angle on his life, Rick Gumble, the owner of a thriving animal hospital in Phoenix, Arizona, began looking for a way to supplement his income. Rick and his wife Dena are true animal lovers, but as Rick started to look at his future, he realized that he had not put enough away for a comfortable retirement. As Rick told Dena, "I don't want to die cleaning out a cat cage." Dena told me, "I didn't understand what Rick was talking about because I loved working at his animal hospital and thought our life was perfect."

But Rick wanted more and found a business that he and Dena could do along with running the animal hospital to bring in the extra income for their future. That was nine years ago. Five years ago, Dena and Rick were making as much from their second business as they were from the animal hospital, so they sold the hospital and turned all their energies into their second business. Today they live on a ten-acre spread with an 1,800-square-foot guest house, two barns, a tack house, eight horses, two llamas, a wallaby, forty-eight exotic birds, various cats and dogs, and a helper to care for the animals. Everything is paid for; there are no mortgages or loans. And, they work about 150 days out of the year taking care of their second business. Rick and Dena knew what they expected from life. That second business didn't happen overnight, but it happened. Didn't it?

Knowing what you expect from life and what you want to contribute to life equips you with the enthusiasm and the magnetism to succeed with shrewd and prosperous decisions. For a quick breakthrough, the following chapter introduces you to old beliefs, many of which are still supported by institutional and governmental policies that have previously suppressed your progress.

As a Result of This Chapter

What do you expect from life?

2

What's Clouding My Thinking?

Results! Why, man, I have gotten a lot of results. I know several thousand things that won't work.

—Thomas A. Edison

Grab something to write on; a legal pad will work. In my workshop entitled Money Management: A State of Mind, I like to start participants off with the following questions. Take a moment to think about the following:

1. When was the last time you felt excited about life?
   - ☐ This morning
   - ☐ Yesterday
   - ☐ Last week
   - ☐ Last month
   - ☐ Last year
   - ☐ Who knows
2. What was it that made you feel excited?

Are your answers anemic little excitements like "I moved the furniture around in my office," "I got to the bottom of that stack of reading," or how about this one: "I found a quicker way home from work"?

Have you been satisfied with the rationale that a little

excitement in your life is all you need to feel credible and useful? Is your maxim, "There's no reason to deviate from what's worked in the past"? Do you let another day slide so you can enjoy one more day of comfort doing what you've always done?

Whose Life Is This Anyhow?

You may have put off grabbing hold of your life in order to enjoy one more day of comfort, but for some that comfort zone has turned into a treadmill as it did for thirty-nine-year-old Tony Spano.

"Everyone thought I should graduate from law school, go to work in my Dad's law firm, get married, and live happily ever after. I knew everyone was expecting me to become a lawyer. After all, my dad was a lawyer," said Tony at one of my workshops. "But I wanted to own a hardware store. I loved working with tools and building things; I built a great tree house and a backboard on our garage for basketball. I love to tinker around and fix things. But when I would bring it up, everyone said, 'Ah, you don't want to do that. What do you know about hardware stores? You'd have to be always out there selling; it takes a special type of person to be a good salesman. That's not your area.' So I just dropped the subject."

Tony had become instilled with fears and limits. He learned to reject new ideas because he feared being disappointed. He chose a safer route. He compromised and accepted things as they were. Today, he wonders why he doesn't have the world by the tail. Tony's story is typical of many of the boomers with whom I have talked. They've lost their passion. They've suppressed their uniqueness. They have learned to color inside the lines.

Coloring Inside the Lines

Your generation's limitations were reinforced by a script that read, "Learning, working, and retirement are stages allocated to particular periods of life, and typically only occur once in a lifetime." Life was highly predictable. Unwittingly, you accepted a criterion that was based on the shorter length of life, analogous to the times of your grandparents—except life is going to be longer for boomers.

Unfortunately, government regulations and institutional rules, supported by economic and medical forecasters, encourage these limitations by telling you when you must be in school, begin your work, and receive your pensions.

The arbitrary nature of this timeline is evident. The age mark of sixty-five for retirement was set merely by a political decision when the Social Security Act was drafted in the 1930s. At that time, life expectancy was only 61.7 years; however, the New Deal congress felt that placing the retirement-benefit age at sixty would make the program too costly. Yet, age seventy would cut out almost everyone, so sixty-five was the reasonable political compromise. Today, when the average life expectancy hovers somewhere around seventy-five and is continually increasing, we live our lives according to this antiquated congressional conclusion. "The economy of the '90s cannot support the dreams of the '60s, let alone the dream of the '30s," former Colorado governor Richard Lamm, told *USA Today.*

The next chapter explores your career options beyond these antiquated conclusions to enhance your position in your field and the quality of life you choose.

As a Result of This Chapter

What outside forces can you think of that you sense have silenced your passion and uniqueness?

3

Redesigning America

To change one's life: Start immediately. Do it flamboyantly. No exceptions.
          —William James

"When we grew up in the '50s and '60s, we were told the world would be our oyster. Now life's turned out to be more of a struggle than we were told it would be," a forty-five-year-old demographer recounted in *Business Week*. But in the '90s, every week thousands of managers, sales executives, lawyers, bankers, accountants, and other professionals are discouraged and angered by the hard realities of the changing world of the workplace. The corporate career was once the solid foundation for millions of middle-class families; it brought them health and pension benefits. But the forces of ardent global competition and industrial consolidation are driving corporations to cut entire layers of middle management and whole categories of professional staff. With corporations no longer rewarding loyalty and performance with lifetime guarantees of employment, many of you find yourselves on the outside alone, afraid, and angry. Don Jordan, a gentleman in his mid-forties told me, "My climb up the occupational ladder has slowed to the point that I feel stuck on a treadmill. I feel like my career and earning power have peaked too soon. I need to get control of my life again."

Your Career Survival Kit

If you are feeling demoralized at the thought of a possible early retirement or layoff, create your own survival tools. These could include:

1. moonlighting to develop a broader portfolio of skills and gain experience in selling yourself directly to customers
2. making contacts on the outside through networking
3. submitting a resumé defining your skills, experience, credentials, or profession with headhunters who know you
4. building a reputation on the outside, perhaps as a specialist in a particular area of your field

This could then head you in several directions, from launching a startup within your own company to discovering your niche within a smaller company, or possibly even changing industries, not an uncommon occurrence.

Perhaps your concern for the environment has shifted your passion to this area of interest. Or, you may have a resumé full of marketable skills and become a professional temp who moves from project to project picking up more marketable skills and expertise.

You may be at that point in your career when it is time for you to go back to school for additional credentials and contacts or take a sabbatical to travel; or, you may want to try working for a particular nonprofit cause about which you are passionate as a volunteer or for a cut in income.

Setting up your own survival kit gives you greater self-esteem and independence which could turn you into a more valuable person to the corporation with which you're already employed.

The Broader Picture of Your Future

What does all this have to do with developing prosperity patterns? Everything! It's all connected to your fiscal success.

As you manage more and more facets of your professional life, the incentive to manage your money naturally evolves. When you take the time to appreciate your uniqueness and to know what you want from your life, you become focused. You become aware of what you are doing with your money and what you want your money to do for you.

The support for this type of belief has become so strong in the medical community that a new field of study has been created called psychoneuroimmunology. In this field we are learning that just thinking vividly about an exciting dream or goal and imagining it as complete with all its benefits can cause our body to create chemicals and hormones which activate our immune system, counter stress, and seem to create new energy, just as if we were experiencing it. Become passionate about life. It stimulates the "can do" in you.

In the following section you'll create your new beginnings by putting on a new set of glasses and exercising mental flexibility through four exercises identified as Workouts. Like a race-car driver who shifts in and out of different gears depending on where he is on the course, you'll learn to shift in and out of different types of thinking.

After completing a Workout, review your responses. Have fun with your answers. Ask: What rules can I break? What's obsolete? Find humor in your approach. After all, you never know where this thinking may lead you.

As a Result of This Chapter

What one unique fact about yourself do you respect the most?
    What has changed for you?

II

Off the Treadmill in Four Workouts

.

4

Workout 1: Coloring Outside the Lines

Argue for your limitations, and sure enough, they're yours.
—Richard Bach

Do What You Love to Do Most

Start the first workout by regressing back in time and then going forward in time. When answering the following questions, don't allow any limitations or judgments to color your answers. Include those fantasies that, when allowed to creep out, cause embarrassment and are quickly suppressed.

Cultivate a zest for change, the type of change that makes it impossible to solve today's problems with yesterday's solutions. Don't even allow the boundaries of this book to restrict you. Use a legal pad instead of the confining space of this book to write down your answers. This time, color outside the lines.

Write down the first thing that comes to mind. Do it quickly. Don't think about it. Enjoy!

1. What do I look forward to the most?
   A. Daily or weekly
   B. Over a year's time
2. What was the most fun for me when I was a child?

3. What do I daydream about when I'm doing what I don't want to do?

- ☐ A. Another profession
- ☐ B. Working at a hobby
- ☐ C. Enjoying a favorite recreation
- ☐ D. Perhaps going to Latvia as an enterprising expert in my field

4. What do I love to do so much that I would do it for free?

5. Visualize that you are a person so renowned in a unique aspect of your industry that you are frequently quoted by *The Today Show* and *Time* magazine. Now, ask yourself: In what unique aspect or particular area of my present career would I enjoy becoming the leading industry specialist or expert?

6. If I knew I would not fail, what would I be doing?

Think over the answers to the above questions. Select the one that creates the greatest excitement. Anything related to your answers is a potential money maker for you. Grab hold of your uniqueness and be assured by what Bette Midler once related: "I didn't belong as a kid, and that always bothered me. If only I'd known that one day my differentness would be an asset, then my early life would have been much easier."

Break With Traditions

Have fun with your answers. Experience the adventure of exposing yourself to something challenging. Define your "differentness" by asking yourself these five questions about your answers to the above questions:

1. What traditions can I break?

2. What's obsolete?

3. What ideas am I in love with that might prevent me from seeing things clearly?

4. Am I asking myself, "How can I make this work?" Or, am I focusing my energy on how it can't work?

5. What is the one thing from the first set of answers that I want to have accomplished when I look back on my life in old age?

Want Something? Go Get It!

Imagine the impetus that motivated the young man in the following story to go after what he wanted with no dread of disapproval, no qualms about treading in empires that most people would consider inaccessible: From the time he was twelve, he dreamed of becoming a leading Hollywood director. At seventeen, his passion took him to Universal Studios on one of those sightseeing tours to which we all have access. But his reasons for taking the tour were different from most. He was there to meet someone who could help him reach his goal to become a movie director. True to his deep commitment to accomplish his purpose, he slipped away from the group and found what he was looking for: a movie being filmed with the crowds of people that it takes to make up a cast and crew. For the rest of the afternoon, he mingled as a member of the crew. From casual conversation he gleaned enough information so that the next day he was able to enter the studio, passing the guard as if he belonged there. On the movie lot, he found an abandoned trailer in which he set up the appearances of an office. Then, he put his name on the door with plastic letters and beneath his name he put the word "Director."

The rest of his summer was spent meeting directors, writers, and editors, learning from every conversation what it takes to become a movie mogul. His every moment was filled with dreams of his life as a movie director, what it would take to become one, what his life would be like from his successes. This was Steven Spielberg.

As a Result of This Chapter

How can I make this work?

What "something" did you discover that you have been withholding which made you weak?

Was it yourself?

5

Workout 2: Vaulting Off Your Treadmill

I never could understand why people paid me so much for doing something I loved to do. But I'll accept their form of appreciation.

—Jay Leno

A recent national poll stated that 95 percent of America's working population do not enjoy the work they do. Those are pretty hefty numbers. How can you enjoy your life if you're bored with your job? It takes up to 80 percent of your life.

Vaulting off your treadmill doesn't necessarily mean finding a new job or starting your own company. A potential money maker may be something you do right now. It may be a unique feature of your present job that you enjoy or in which you are interested. Real innovators derive personal satisfaction from making a difference. It may be an outside interest, or it may be something you have wanted to attempt but haven't taken the time to pursue.

Determining Your Area of Expertise

The trick is to learn that if you look differently at something you like, you can find a way to make it pay. Determine what one area of your corporation or your career you really enjoy and become an expert in that area, or become a crack golfer, a skillful artist, or a volunteer. This could lead to good contacts for your existing position, the introduction to a new position, or even the start of a new business. You may want to start diversifying your income ability by starting a new business after hours. That way, you can slowly become familiar with your new adventure before you break off from the security of your previous career.

Winning Starts With Beginning

To begin including what you love to do in your life today, settle into a place where you feel particularly comfortable, a favorite writing desk or someplace you find nurturing. I have an eighteen-year-old oversized Queen Anne chair I like to hang over when I'm reading or getting my head organized. To complete your workout:

1. Start by describing exactly what you want. In other words, identify your goal, complete with all its benefits.
2. How would you feel if you became a master or expert in any area you enjoy?
3. What benefits would this achievement bring?
4. Think about someone who's already enjoying the results you want to attain. What exceptional qualities does that person have that you value?
5. Write down the general steps needed to reach your goal of doing what you love to do.
6. Peruse each general step. Describe the specific steps you will take to make what you love to do your goal.
7. Write down a specific action you can take today as the first step toward making what you love to do your goal.

Mine your unconscious for clues. Discipline yourself to keep a journal, record your dreams, write an autobiography. The process should be regular but unstructured, without any rules as to content and style. Imagine the shape of your ideal life one year from today, then work backward to formulate a series of goals that will take you there. When you define your vision, the desire to direct your money toward your vision follows.

In order to develop staying power, you need to understand what incentives you possess that back your commitments. In the next chapter you will learn that it is your values that control your incentives and direct your commitments toward or away from your success.

As a Result of This Chapter

What unique thoughts confronted you which exposed your own reality?

6

Workout 3: Commitments and Other Lofty Words

If you don't ask 'Why this?' often enough, somebody will ask 'Why you?'
— Tom Hirshfield, inventor

Take yourself back in time to the dismal gloom and doom years of the Depression. You are in a bank. You know, the kind in the 1930s movies with the high ceilings, pretentious columns, and grave wood-paneled walls, where everyone speaks in hushed, secretive tones. To one side, a slim, ordinary looking man with dark hair and a pencil moustache sits in front of a pompous, overfed loan officer. Suddenly, the intimidating silence is broken. The loan officer bellows incredulously, "You've got to be kidding, Mr. Disney! You want three million dollars for a mouse! I can draw a mouse!"

Today, anything with the word Disney in front of it produces visions of success. The memory of the tune "When You Wish Upon a Star" inspires thoughts of the Magic Castle, Peter Pan flying through the sky, horse-drawn street cars clanking down streets from the turn of the twentieth century, Space Mountain, Indiana Jones, and a man whose life was committed to the creative spirit. With his creative mind, Walt Disney visualized cartoons, movies, and entertainment parks to lure people into taking time out to refresh their minds and hearts. Then he went one step further. He envisioned and developed plans for a park with the purpose of stimulating his audiences' creative spirit. He created Epcot Center.

Walt Disney knew what he loved to do. He could visualize turning what he loved to do into realities and imagined his dreams with all their benefits. In his mind he accepted the responsibility for the accomplishment of his dreams. He wasn't a master cartoonist, so he hired the best. He didn't have the money, so he went to those who did, and kept asking until he got it. He knew he needed someone to help him manage his ambition, so he brought his brother, Roy, and his father into the business.

Walt Disney wasn't the first person to have these visions nor the last, but he was committed to his vision, to his uniqueness, and to his creativity. Commitment comes from knowing you will accomplish what you set out to do before you do it. You are willing to accept the responsibility for the accomplishment of your goal and the consequences along the way.

The Teenager's Commitment

To what, in your life, have you been so committed that you knew beforehand you would absolutely accomplish your endeavor before you did it and would unequivocally accept the consequences along the way? For Judy Siegel, a Los Angeles bank executive, it was when she was a teenager, waiting to learn how to drive a car. "By the time I got that learner's permit, even though I had never been behind the wheel, I knew I was going to be able to drive that car. For months I had been mentally driving that car all over town. I absolutely knew all I needed was a little practice." Judy definitely pictured her dream and imagined all its benefits.

When you were learning to drive, did you give a second thought to all the possible consequences which that commitment to driving a car would bring you? Were you hung up worrying about all the problems that could possibly occur? I doubt many of us let the thought of possible problems enter our minds. Learning to drive that car was our liberation. The consequences of the commitment to drive that car were, in our minds, challenges for us, not problems. We could do it. In order to rekindle the magnitude of passion of that commitment, put your values in line with the goals and objectives you visualize.

Disagreeing Values

What does this mean? Much of the struggle that people experience in life results from conflicting values. Conflicting values obstruct our decision-making process and lead us off the track. We must understand that our values need to be compatible with the goals and objectives we visualize.

What we choose to do depends on what we place as our highest value at the time. The freedom we felt from knowing how to drive that car was more important to us than the peace of mind and security we could have had taking a bus and letting someone else take the responsibility. In fact, being able to drive a car was so important to us that, in our minds, it gave us peace and security. We felt we were now self-reliant.

When you understand how you prioritize your values, then you'll understand why you do certain things, and why other people do what they do.

Prioritizing Values

Sorting out your values is your goal in this workout; defining those beliefs in life that are most important to you. Go through the following list once or twice, and write down those values that seem important to you.

Having fun	Growth
Peace of mind	Love
Spiritual harmony	Financial security

Free personal time	Loyalty to old friends
Power	Sincerity
Health and fitness	Honesty
Wealth	Respect
Adventure	Time with your family
Challenge	Creativity
Money	Community service
Environmental issues	Spouse relationship

If you think of other values that are important to you and are not listed here, jot them down.

Now, prioritize those values you have listed from the most important to the least important. Start at the top of the list. For instance, peace of mind is a value we all want, but is it more important to you than financial security? Is financial security more important than taking on a new challenge? Is being with your family more important than power but less important than money? Is your loyalty to friends more important than your growth? Others can stop you temporarily, but only you can do it permanently. Are old traditions, like after-work drinks, more important than creative time? Consciously or unconsciously, you always get what you expect. Get to know who you are. The more specific you are about your definitions, the more you'll learn about yourself, such as defining what fun means to you.

Prioritize your value list to reflect the way you honestly feel, not the way others' values have biased your beliefs. If you don't like what you see, make a second goal list of values; in other words, create a list of values toward which you would like to strive. Think about these values often. You cannot decide upon a course of action or inaction unless your values have been clearly identified.

Share this chapter with your family. Have a lively discussion with them about values. Ask them about their values and what their values mean to their lives personally. Tell them what you are about. Encourage them to take time to examine their values. Ask them if their values today will help them in the future.

Your values change over time, so make this chapter a part of your life and use it to propel you past confusing times. Understanding your values helps you to act upon your life rather than react. When we accept responsibility for our actions, we are taking that first step toward doing more than just surviving.

As a Result of This Chapter

Why did you learn to drive?

What special knowledge did you grasp which energized your commitment?

7

Workout 4: Capitalize on Your Resources

The way I see it, if you want the rainbow, you gotta put up with the rain.

—Dolly Parton

The Pain of Change Is Mainly in the Brain

At the thought of major change, are you overcome by pain and confusion brought upon by the fear of the unknown? Success begins in the mind, but negative subconscious memories often stall your attempts to develop such habits. These memories elicit pain that provokes you into procrastinating. They need erasing or editing to work in your favor. Your goal is to shift away from your negative subconscious memories by focusing on an optimistic tomorrow, the tomorrow you have designed for yourself.

Your Values Directing Your Life's Design

In this workout you will bring together the things you love to do and your values by merging them into your life's design. Your aim is to develop your goals through the following eight insightful steps.

26

1. Across the top of your legal pad sketch five columns and install the following five headings: By Friday, by the end of this month, in six months, in one year, in five years.

2. Down the left side of your legal pad write the following categories: Family, Money Management, Community, Business, Recreation.

3. Under the time frames, put your goals for each category.

4. Looking back at your list of values, write a paragraph describing how your values are compatible with these time-frame goals. If you find your values are not compatible with these goals, describe how they conflict. What is your solution?

5. Compose a paragraph on how you perceive things will be when you have completed your visions. What possible effects will completing your visions have on your life? What possible consequences will be involved? Are you willing to accept the responsibility for those consequences?

6. Now write about the distress you will feel if you do not accomplish your objectives.

7. Finally, again write down the specific action you are going to take today to start your progress toward your goals.

8. Go out and do step seven.

Congratulations! Now you are ready to learn how your subconscious is a catalyst to the successful attainment of your visions. In the following chapter you'll develop your mental awareness list that becomes your subconscious commitment to your success.

As a Result of This Chapter

What one thing can you see leading you toward a lasting solution to your conflicts?

What has changed for you?

III

Jump-Start the Quality of Your Life

8

So Start Here Now

Do what you can, with what you have, where you are.
—Theodore Roosevelt

Watching a professional basketball player in the heat of a game pass the ball to a teammate while seemingly not looking doesn't happen because the player has eyes in the back of his head or was just lucky. In the book *Show Time,* author Pat Riley, who has one of the most successful careers as a coach of National Basketball Association champions, tells us it is practicing so often that lets the players act from knowing and feel free to open their senses to make such winning moves. In other words, they do not have to concentrate on how they are going to throw the ball or worry if the teammate is going to be there. They know from practice how to execute the play automatically, and can now rely on their senses to confirm that their teammate is where he is expected to be to complete the drive.

Success here means generating pleasure from what you are doing. The athlete derives pleasure from winning. The professional has practiced the right moves for so long that the conscious thinking process is not required. The correct winning responses are automatic, a habit. All athletes are aware that the winners are the ones who defeat themselves the least.

31

In the following section you learn the conscious moves that become automatic, subconscious actions which will help you manage money and create a wealth consciousness.

How the Smart Money Gets That Way

Sit back in your chair for a moment and think about the last social situation in which you were involved when someone started discussing money. I'm talking about the people who appear to have their financial act together. Have you ever noticed how they love to boast about the latest investment recommendation they got from their stockbroker, or better yet, how they found a new way to save on their taxes? Mention either of these subjects and their eyes light up like the Las Vegas strip at midnight. It's like a game to them.

The game starts with a mental-awareness list which they practiced over and over, just like professional athletes practice their game over and over, until it becomes second nature.

The financially successful have linking questions that have become part of their subconscious minds. These questions became a part of their thinking processes through the conscious habit of reviewing a mental awareness list. That mental awareness list includes these questions:

- What do you want from life?
- How can I accumulate money effortlessly?
- How can I position my money to work harder for me?
- What is costing me money?

These questions are constantly asked in their subconscious minds and are fine tuned by their conscious minds daily. In order to launch yourself into this list of questions with extraordinary momentum, start by first recognizing and being thankful for everything you already have in your life.

Don't worry about the things you don't think you have; focus on all the things you do have, and smile. Now combine the things-you-have list with your lists from the exercises in Part II.

They constitute the answer for the first question on your mental awareness list: "What do I want from life?"

The next question on the mental awareness list is "How can I accumulate money more readily?" When I say this to most people, they counter with, "How can I accumulate money, period?" Answer: Pay yourself first.

This program works on the same basis as your rent or mortgage payment. You pay yourself first, every month at the beginning of the month, by sending a check to a growth mutual fund. In this program it's not the amount but the regularity that counts. Start with as little as $25, but start. Your goal is 10 percent of your after-tax income. Type up a bill for yourself titled Pay Me First, and stick it on top of your stack of bills. Treat it as your first necessity. Pogo, the comic strip character created by Walt Kelly, put it this way: "We have met the enemy and they is us."

MUTUAL FUND

An investment trust in which your dollars are pooled with those of thousands of other investors in a diversified portfolio of stocks and/or bonds with the guidance of a professional manager. In this way, the investor can profit without shouldering alone the burden of risk. In this case, the investment is in stock.

A growth fund, or stock fund as it is also called, invests in the stocks of our country's larger, established companies with the potential for long-term capital appreciation.

It is very easy and comfortable to say, "I am going to do this program but I can't afford it right now." It's like I am going to start my diet next Monday; there is always a reason to start it another Monday. It is in fact important to start your Pay Me First program right now, immediately, "even as we speak," to quote NBC's weatherman, Willard Scott.

But why?

Compounding Euphoria

How does a half million bucks, more or less, sound? In the following scenario a difference of ten years means $677,121.

The Adamses, a thirty-six-year-old couple, and the Carters, a forty-six-year-old couple, have decided to deposit $4,000 into an Individual Retirement Account (IRA) at the beginning of each year until age sixty-five. They are investing in a stock mutual fund which has a good steady record averaging a 12 percent total return for the past twenty-five years, so let's assume it will continue to do this. They intend to reinvest their earnings as in the previous example. The question is how much will they have when they reach age 65?

| thirty-six-year-old couple | $965,331 |
| forty-six-year-old couple | $288,210 |

"As with the Theory of Relativity, most are familiar with the term compounding but don't realize its astounding results."

—Albert Einstein

To comprehend what happens when your money is compounding, think of it as mixing a fine martini—three parts gin to one part vermouth. The earnings (interest, dividends, and/or capital gains) are mixed with the initial money you deposited. Breaking the formula down to its simplest use, assume the following:

Your initial deposit is:	$4,000
The earnings equal a rate	
of 12% annually:	× 12%
Which equals:	$ 480

Now mix the initial deposit with your earnings, and your balance for the year is $4,480. Big deal! The second year you leave the entire $4,480 in the same 12 percent fund. At the end of that year you now have $5,018. At the end of five years your fund account is worth $7,049, not quite double. Stay with me on this. Eventually, it grows at a wild and crazy pace.

With compounding, money does not grow at the same rate forever. If you needed your money in ten years, you would have $12,423. From simply investing $4,000 and reinvesting the earnings your initial deposit has now more than tripled. As long as the earnings are reinvested, the longer it is held, the faster it grows. At thirty years, from that one single investment of $4,000 and your commitment, you would have $119,840. Some martini!

Pay Me First is your first step to breaking procrastination's grip without feeling overwhelmed. For further analysis of compounding, see Appendix A for a Compounded Rate of Return Matrix.

Even As We Speak

Start small: Grab a 5 × 8 card, a red crayon, marking pen, or nail polish, and print in big kindergarten letters: Pay Me First. Tape that directive to your morning mirror. Make sure it gets in the way of that good-looking puss of yours so you remember to read it aloud each time you see it. Don't worry about what your roommate, family, or significant other thinks. Your business is to make Pay Me First a way of life and to know the reason why.

Start right now with making that card and taping it on the mirror. Do not read the next paragraph. It will be here when you get back.

Now make up a bill which states the exact amount you are going to pay yourself and the address of the mutual fund to which you are going to send it. Some mutual funds will take an amount as low as $25 as long as you use an automatic investment plan. You activate this service by authorizing the fund company to draw on your bank account regularly by check. If $25 is all you can initially afford, don't be discouraged by thinking it is so little. Instead focus on the fact that it is the most important $25 of your life; it is the start of your new money management habits. Don't forget to put a reminder on your calendar in red ink; starting a new habit takes a lot of support for follow-through.

Mark on your calendar exactly when you will reach your goal of putting 10 percent of your income away. Make this date no later than thirteen weeks from today.

Commit to writing a promise to yourself that you will never touch that money, not for overdue bills, emergencies, or any other pressing reason, because this is your commitment money to your new financial confidence. You have immediately boosted your can-do spirit: You now see yourself as an investor, someone who is making choices about how his or her money is spent. You have ceased reacting to others' values.

Next, copy down the mental awareness list of codes and put them on your nightstand so you can review them each morning upon waking and each evening just before you turn out the light.

The next chapter continues your search for how you can accumulate more money and position your money to work harder for you.

As a Result of This Chapter

What incentives do you have to consistently pursue the exercises presented in this chapter?

9

Dumping Your Debt

Try? There is no try. There is only do or not do.
　　　　　　　—Yoda, in *The Empire Strikes Back*

Pay off your credit cards and earn 30 percent on this riskless investment. What? How so? If you pay 31 percent in federal tax, 12 percent in state tax, and 12 percent interest with after-tax dollars on your credit card, you'd have to find an investment earning 34.6 percent that would pay you as much as you'd save by paying down your credit card balance.

Shifting the Odds in Your Favor

Your first goal is debt control. Here are some good common-sense guidelines to advance you toward your goals:

- Allocate no more than 65 percent of your after-tax income for fixed monthly expenses (food, utilities, and housing).
- Allot only 10 percent for installment debt (cars, furniture, appliances).
- If you have a savings account earning 5.5 percent, raid it and pay off your credit cards. You are never going to get ahead when your installment loans and credit card interest cost you three times that much.

- Treat all spending of money as a business transaction; that is, apply a cost-to-benefit analysis. Ask yourself, "What will it cost me in work hours versus what I will get?" When you are looking at the price, don't forget to add in the consumer tax and remember you are paying with after-tax dollars.
- Look to pay raises, windfalls, bonuses, gifts, tax refunds, freelance fees, and profits from your investments as a way of getting off the interest payment treadmill.

Your second goal is credit planning. Establish as high a personal line of credit as you can get the banks to give you. Leave it there and use it only for strategic purposes, such as:

- for an extra emergency fund, so you can raise the deductibles on your health insurance, car, and house insurance, thereby lowering your premiums;
- for investments, so you can write off the interest when you borrow for investments;
- for bridge loans, in case you need the down payment for your new home now and your present home is in escrow. Be sure you have enough money to carry the two mortgages in case your present home falls out of escrow.

Use an equity line of credit on your home to pay off your credit cards and car loans so you can write off the interest against your taxes. Then pay your equity line of credit off.

Throw your credit cards in your drawer and think of them as if they are a part of your line of credit for your credit planning.

The Nineties: The Age of Autonomy

The definition for autonomous is "existing or functioning independently; having self-government or home rule." Your home rule is to think of your credit cards and credit lines as a way to function independently. Think of your credit as a way to help you get away from low-producing savings accounts and low deductibles on your insurance. When you think of credit as your cushion for emergencies only and not as extra lump sums of money to buy a more extravagant lifestyle, you now have the freedom to earn higher returns on your money.

The aim of your generation for the nineties is value for your money. That's why stores like the Price Club, BJ's Wholesale Club, and discount shopping centers are blooming across our country. People are tired of paying designer prices, but they still want the designer merchandise. Breaking the credit card habit is like trying to go on a diet. Taking the time to put your intentions in writing and reviewing them once a week or more reinforces your commitment. To jump-start your new outlook, start by enumerating the credit objectives you wish to accomplish this year. Then, write a sentence describing your commitment to achieving these goals and why, followed by a sentence or two on what positive effects will result. Continue by asking yourself, "How will I feel when I accomplish my expectations?" and, "What will I lose if I do not accomplish my goals?"

As a Result of This Chapter

What one thing did you learn that is important to your future financial success?

10

Reversing the Odds in Your Favor

By identifying the forces pushing the future, rather than those that have contained the past, you possess the power to engage with your reality.

—*Megatrends 2000* by John Naisbitt
and Patricia Aburdene

Just like the word "diet," if you use the word budget all you can think about are feelings of being restricted and deprived. "Budget? No way! Period! I haven't worked my tail off to have to be restricted by a budget. Budgets are like diets; no one ever stays on a diet."

However, when the word diet was no longer used, and the same eating suggestions were touted as resources for keeping fit to lead an active life, we shifted our mental attitude. We now eat more vegetables, fruits, and consciously reduce our intake of fat because we want to lead healthier lives. We no longer feel deprived. We choose which foods we want to eat, not which foods we can't eat. When we do reach for the Haagen Dazs, we're aware of our selection and compensate for it with other nonfat food selections and exercise. If you shift your attitude and think of money management as a way to analyze how to have your money serve you better, you can get more for your buck.

Your Money's Modus Operandi

"What is costing me money?" The last question in your mental awareness list requires finding out how your money has been serving you in the past. Some assembly on your part is required.

Step One:If you have a significant other, sit him or her down. With legal pad and pencil in hand, put your heads together and write down all the things you own with their approximate values down the left side of the pad. Then write everything you owe and ballpark amounts on the right side of the pad. Subtract what you owe from what you own, and that is your net worth. Which list totals more? MY/OUR NET WORTH _____

Step Two: On the next sheet of your legal pad, jot down your sources of income on the left hand side. In the middle of the page, log in the dollar amounts from these sources for the year. Then, tally up your incomes and record the amounts on the far right hand side of the page. TOTAL INCOME _____

Step Three: On the next sheet, document how your income was disbursed. Determine monthly expenditures by averaging three months of data.

A good way to get your bearings on this is to grab your last year's check register and chart the various categories it relays: medical, entertainment, housing, food, etc. There will be a category called miscellaneous because there were moneys doled out that are not documented. Use the same format as above, and then add up your disbursements and write the amounts on the far right hand side of the page. TOTAL OUTGO _____

Step Four: On the next sheet of paper write down all three totals: net worth, total income, total outgo.

Step Five: Write a one-sentence summary about how you feel about your totals. How far are you from your goals?

Step Six: This next question is important. It is designed to aid you in gaining the greatest amount of benefit from the following section. What concerns did you have after you read your totals? Understand your feelings; write them down. If you feel like a

Mack truck with two flat tires in the far left lane on an L.A. freeway, elaborate on these feelings until you are motivated to become intent on finding out what costs you money. Become so dissatisfied that you visualize yourself jumping out of that truck and stopping the freeway traffic until you can maneuver yourself out of your turmoil.

Step Seven: Project this month's cash flow based on past expenses. Determine if each expenditure is put toward what you value, what your goals are, and what is important to you. If it's not, ask yourself, "What purpose does spending it serve?"

Profit From Dissatisfaction

If you were dissatisfied, you can redirect your energy to get control of where your income is circulated. Right now take a look at your miscellaneous expenditures. Take the time to think about where the moneys went in that category. Consider your use of that handy little machine I call the candy machine, better known in banking circles as the automatic teller machine (ATM).

Cash? Where did that cash go? How many spontaneous purchases a week do you make "for the fun of it"? Are you spending money on material "status symbols"? Do you go out for a drink after work every night? Out to lunch? Out to dinner? Did you buy some cute little gadget to make everyone in the office laugh? Ask yourself: Which of these provides more lasting value in my life? What could be eliminated? How you spend and save your money reflects your deepest personal values, your goals, and what you think is important.

How Much Do We Really Understand?

Here's an eye-opening exercise for you to get a quick handle on your spontaneous spending habits:

   1. Make a list every night of the way you expect to spend your

money for the next day. List what your money is purchasing and what you expect you will spend.

2. During the day, unless something is on that list, don't buy it.

3. To get a real feeling for exactly what that means in real dollars, document the purchases, lunches, and drinks that you passed up to stay on this exercise, total the amount of money you saved, and toss that amount of money into a jar.

4. At the end of the week, check what you have in that jar. Try it for a week.

You'll like it. You'll like the feel of all that money at the end of the week. You might like it so much that it will inspire you to look more closely at the other categories. Be sure to document how much you saved so you can feel proud of yourself. Now deposit these savings in a mutual fund, or, if you owe anything on your credit cards, start dumping that debt.

It will realistically take you about thirteen weeks to pinpoint and make adjustments to the way your money is serving you. It takes time to discover where some of those overlooked expenditures are and even more time to develop and readjust your spending focus. For now, some housekeeping is in order.

Dealing With Dangerous Money Difficulties

In most couples, to varying degrees, one person is a spender and the other is a saver. A lot of resentment piles up when you feel you can't or don't communicate about how the money is spent; one or both feel their opinions are not being respected. If you feel this is a particular problem in your situation, there is a book by psychologist Victoria Felton-Collins, entitled *Couples and Money,* which may be of help to you.

On a more stressful note, if you are looking at house payments alone that are 40 percent of your after-tax income and car payments that are 15 percent of said income, you will need to win the lottery to get you out of debt. You may want to get some professional assistance. For a nonprofit credit counseling organization near you, write to the National Foundation for Consumer Credit, 8701 Georgia Ave., Silver Spring, MD 20910. The National Foundation for Consumer Credit is funded by banks, department stores, labor groups, legal organizations, and other businesses. Your business with the NFCC is treated confidentially. The initial consultation costs between $10 and $50, and a debt payment plan will cost about $15 a month. A debt payment plan, if necessary, will require you to give the agency an amount equal to one-thirtieth of the total amount you owe each month. The counselor will also work with your creditors.

As a Result of This Chapter

What is the first action you will take today to implement your understanding of how your money was spent?

11

Personal Paper Panic

*A tree as big around as you can reach starts with a small seed;
a thousand-mile journey starts with one small step.*

—Lao-Tse

Imagine this nightmare: It is 2:00 in the morning; you're at the bottom of a 600-room hotel laundry shoot submerged in the confines of an enormous laundry basket. The downpour of sheets is constant; you're suffocating from their weight. Overwrought with confusion, you frantically battle through the tangled mess hoping to reach the top of the basket. Finally, you can visualize climbing out of the basket when suddenly the deluge starts again. The oppressive weight of the sheets immobilizes you; your breath is smothered and as your mind slips into a dizzying fog, you find yourself in an enormous ice-white room fleeing from the sheets, dodging mounds of bills, shunning masses of unanswered letters, uncompleted reports, unbalanced bank statements, articles to read, and piles and heaps of data to be filed. Suddenly, your anxiety bolts you out of your sleep when you see they all have your name on them.

Ruts, Gullies, and Habits

Life's continual battle of getting the everyday blight of bills,

letters, junk mail, and personal business in order is a major
distraction when one is attempting to get on with his financial
life. Facing an out-of-control work space is a leading cause of
procrastination. What to save? Where to save it? What to throw
away? Unless that work space of yours is cleared, it is not a work
space; it's a catch-all that boggles your mind. It defeats your
enthusiasm rather than enticing you to sit down and work on
being more creative with your life. Hence, back to the
treadmill.

This chapter introduces routines and filing systems to reduce
the hassle of dealing with your personal business, with particular emphasis on how to document your tax information.

The Third Fact of Life: The Mail

They (whoever "they" are) say there are two facts of life that
none of us can escape: death and taxes. This is a little short
sighted. There are three facts of life that none of us can escape:
death, taxes, and the mail. When you think about it, the mail is
much more aggravating than death and taxes. Death is a once-
in-a-lifetime thing, and taxes are a periodic occurrence. The
mail is ongoing, nagging at you day in, day out.

Some people just throw it in the corner and let it stack up for
years until their relatives or neighbors call the fire department.
They're the lucky ones. But, for most of us, this would just add
to our list of anxieties; we'd be incessantly worrying about what
disparaging messages our landlord or mortgage lender, the IRS,
and the like were sending us.

If you've ever read an article on organization or attended one
of those seminars like "How I Became the Wealthiest Person in
the World Through Time Management," you have heard "Handle your mail only once." This is how it works: After you open
your mail, do not put it back in the envelope.

Date it, paper clip it, and then toss it in one of the
appropriate baskets, which are titled Bills to Pay, Things to Do,
and Things to File.

Every two weeks, go through the baskets and pay your bills, do your paperwork, and get your filing out of the way. It becomes a comfortable routine because you choose when you are going to take care of what you have to do, and therefore don't feel the pain of it constantly nagging at you day in, day out.

Caution: If one of your bills doesn't fall due in this scenario, and there is one in every crowd, either enter its "late date" seven days earlier on your calendar in red ink or just pay it and get it out of your hair.

When it comes to your things-to-do basket, if you're not careful, it can become overwhelming. Date the material as you put it in the basket, and if it's still there thirty days later, toss it, calendar it, or file it.

Randomly Among the Mess, Simplified

To get started you'll need a few essentials. Don't worry about getting fancy; just grab whatever is around the house or in your neighbor's garage.

- Find three boxes about 10 × 15 inches into which to toss your mail. Label one Bills to Pay, one Things to Do, and one Things to File.
- Clean out your desk's file drawer; you're going to use it to hold files. If you don't have a file drawer, find a sturdy box which can serve this purpose.
- You'll need a calculator, preferably one with a tape, kept at your work space and not hauled around the house or to the office.
- At your work space, where you can easily see it each day, place a calendar that has large spaces under each day in which to write reminders. Use your calendar for everything on your mind: Chores you have to do, appointments and dates, special projects you've been meaning to tackle, and nice things to remember like birth and anniversary dates, and friends to call. Don't forget to include calls to your mom and dad.

- Keep a personal telephone directory. It can be a rolling card file, an index card box, or a book to which you can add new pages. If you use a book, enter the information with a pencil so you don't have to rewrite the whole directory every three years.
- From the local save-a-buck office supply store, pick up an array of office essentials: Cellophane tape, stapler, ruler, the usual. Get the same supplies for the kitchen drawer and the garage workbench. You can also find a file box there.

Question: What do you do with all those papers you're afraid of losing? Pull out your file box and tab it off into three sections:

- Important Papers
- "Stuff"
- Taxes

Now you're ready for some serious time-management organization.

As a Result of This Chapter

What are the biggest changes you will make from what you learned in this chapter to help expedite your enterprising attributes?

12

Positioning the Offense

Finally you understand that the real motorcycle you're working on is yourself.

—Robert M. Pirsig, *Zen and the Art of Motorcycle Maintenance*

Re: Important Papers

Most of the time we aren't interested in our important papers, but when we need them and can't find them, our anxiety level drives us to the brink of hysteria. Many a good day and some outstanding relationships have been ruined because of the loss of an important document.

We can make lists all day and night about what should be considered "important" papers; however, in the interest of the more intriguing subject matter to be read in this book, I'll keep the subject headings to a few general information topics:

- your goals from your workouts
- auto: include leases, buyer's agreements, and loan documents
- casualty insurance: include documents for properties, autos, and recreational items, and broker's name and phone number on inside left cover

- life insurance policies: include broker's name and phone number on inside left cover, policies, and any correspondence
- health insurance and disability policies: include the name and phone number of the broker and an insurance claim log on the left inside cover which contains the treatment date, the treatment, treatment cost, and who billed you, the date the claim was sent to the insurer, reimbursement amount received and date, net cost to you, any pertinent phone calls you made and with whom you talked
- investment files with a heading for each investment: include a log on the left inside cover which contains the date and time you bought your investment, name of person from whom you bought it and her or his telephone number, what you bought or sold with address, account number, number of shares purchased, and price paid
- medical records: include blood type and names of doctors
- guarantees and product information
- records: include birth certificates, marriage documents, social security data, passports, voter registrations
- career information and resumés
- wills and trusts
- property files by address—the file label should read 123 Main Street, Anytown, State: include escrow and loan documents, and improvement bills
- credit information
- retirement plan documents—the file label should read: IRA—XYZ mutual fund, or 401(k) plan—company name or Profit Sharing Plan—documents and investments
- banking relationships: include the name of the loan officer you know well enough to get a quick loan—more in chapter 7
- loans to others—the file label should read: Loan Document—Re: Dick Jones
- letters of instruction: include funeral instructions, living will, people to notify, will and trust location, safety deposit

box location and key, and name of attorney and financial
advisor
- important relatives file or "Mom": include telephone numbers of close neighbors, friends, and doctors, and any
business information they are willing to share with you.

Re: Stuff

"When you fly over any big city you will see rows and rows of
houses. If you look closely you will realize that the rows of
houses are really only rows and rows of boxes for us to keep our
stuff in." So goes the beginning of George Carlin's comedy
routine on people and their stuff. It's a great routine that leaves
you in tears of laughter and wanting to throw everything out
except your toothbrush. But stuff we have, and, being human, it
is stuff we love.

For now, throw it all in a box marked "stuff" and set it aside
for when you're watching television. Mark on your calendar
when you should have your "stuff" files completed so they will
be out of your way in sixty days.

What goes into the "stuff" files? If you didn't file it under the
heading "important papers" and you don't need it for the IRS, it
can be filed here. Be sure to look around your home and at the
office for "stuff" that can be filed away here, such as:

- letters from some of your favorite people (If you are keeping
letters from not-so-favorite people they should be filed in
the "important papers" section or thrown out. Get the
negative "stuff" out of your life.)
- copies of letters to your favorite people
- articles about things of interest
- travel ideas
- restaurants you want to try out
- cartoons you enjoy
- things you want to do some day
- health articles or booklets

Learn to let go. Be selective about the papers you keep, particularly where mementos are concerned. Remember that eighty percent of everything you file you will never look at again.

As a Result of This Chapter

In what way will this chapter allow you to enlarge your consciousness?

13

Keeping Good Tax Records

They always say that time changes things, but you actually have to change them yourself.

—Andy Warhol

At tax time, instead of yanking out the back seat of your car, going through your closets, drawers, and sports bags looking frantically for those receipts and records necessary to lower that bottom line on your tax return, Jim Houle, a CPA in Orange, California, has developed a simplified set of forms for his clients to disclose their tax picture to him each year. Using Jim's guidelines, here is an easy filing system which will enable you to have your records organized and ready to go. All you'll have to do at the end of the year is pull these files out and hand them over to your tax advisor. To save some money, you may want to take a couple of hours to add everything up. It's not necessary; it's up to you.

The System

This system will make you think you've died and gone to heaven; it's easy and informative. Grab ten clean files and label them as follows:

- Bank Receipts
- Bank Statements and Canceled Checks
- Information
- Income
- Adjustments to Income
- Dividends/Capital Gains and Interest Income
- Itemized Deductions
- Business Income and Expenses
- Rental Income and Expenses
- Employee Business Expenses

If you think that some of these files don't relate to you, label them anyway as goal reminders toward building your financial visions.

Tip: Take this book to your nearest copying machine, reproduce your own set of the lists found in Appendix B and place the pages inside the appropriate files. If you are filing jointly and you are both employed, make two copies of the Employee Business Expenses sheet.

A Point or Two About "The System"

After you have set up your files, just drop all your tax information, receipts, documents, and notes in the appropriate file. When in doubt, review the forms you inserted in the files; they tell the story. Or you can pitch the information into the Information file with a note to your tax advisor as to why there is so much confusion.

There are five time scenarios you can choose from to compile this material: Each month, quarterly, semi-annually, at the end of the year, or let your tax advisor bill you for his or her time for compiling your information.

If you follow the system, you can compile the information in these files while watching the evening news and a sitcom or two.

Now that you have your tax reporting organized, let's take a

.

look at the five major areas that cost you money, starting with taxes.

As a Result of This Chapter

What component of this chapter will be of the greatest value to you in aiding you toward your goals?

What has changed for you?

IV

What Costs You Money

14

The Second Fact of Life: Taxes

To the degree we're not living our dreams, our comfort zone has more control of us than we have over ourselves.

—Do It! Let's Get Off Our Buts by
John-Roger and Peter McWilliams

"My taxes are cut and dried, so I only need to file a short form...Tax strategies only save me a buck or two...Reducing your taxes is cheating!" If these are your laments, think again.

One-third of all the money you accumulate belongs to the Internal Revenue Service. Or does it? What you may or may not know is that the amount of income tax for which you are liable has little to do with your total income. It has everything to do with your knowledge of tax strategies.

You read every day how the very wealthy pay little in the way of taxes. What they actually do is spend and accumulate their money with the knowledge of positive, legal great tax strategies for every dollar with which they come in contact. Those who fill out the short form are paying the absolute maximum tax which can be paid on their income.

If you think you don't have more than the standard deduction, the long form will point out where you can improve your tax planning. Use the long form; you can only pay less in taxes. Worst case: you'll pay the same this year but have new knowledge of tax deductions for which you can aim next year.

Use It or Lose It

One of the best ways to save money is to become savvy about your taxes. For instance, good habits result in deductions for your income, assets, and expenses which gives you more money to put toward your aspirations. Don Perkins, an accountant in San Diego, California, suggests that you consider these two examples:

1. If you are an employee and your income is $60,000, you are paying a combined federal and state tax of 35 percent. This equals $21,000. Question: How do you lower your tax bill?

A. Take advantage of retirement plans (IRAs, 401(k) plans, Keoghs, etc.). They give you an immediate tax savings, plus, your investment will grow more quickly because it is tax-sheltered (not taxed until you withdraw the money).

B. Start your own business doing what you love to do. Any ordinary and necessary expenses incurred in connection with that business will be deductible and will help to lower your tax. At the same time, you will be working toward your goal of having your own business.

2. If you are self-employed and you don't save receipts from your business expenses, you are throwing a lot of money away. For instance, on a $1,000.00 accumulation of business expenses, you could be throwing away $480.00.

28 %	Federal Tax
5 %	State (2–7% average)
15.3%	Social Security Tax
48.3%	Total Tax

Eight Good Tax-Fighting Habits

"There is no expedient to which a person will not go to avoid the real labor of thinking," commented Thomas Edison in 1929. But the truth is, most of us do look for positive habits to improve our quality of life. And that takes introspection. Here's how you can quickly create eight new habits to save you dollars:

Habit 1: Change your thinking that reducing your taxes is cheating. Understand the difference between tax cheating and tax strategies.

Tax cheating includes understating your income, claiming tax deductions for assets you don't own, and claiming expenditures you never made which result in anything from high penalties to jail sentences.

Tax strategies are legal uses of the tax laws to reduce your income taxes. These include opening an IRA account, starting a small business, taking advantage of 401(k) plans and pension and profit sharing plans, buying real estate, entertaining and traveling on tax deductible dollars, and many more.

The legality and morality of tax deductions was settled over forty-five years ago by the United States Circuit Court of Appeals in an opinion written by Judge Learned Hand that read, "Anyone may so arrange his affairs that his taxes shall be as low as possible. He is not bound to choose a pattern that will best pay the treasury. No one owes any public duty to pay more than the law demands."

Rearranging how you earn and spend your money to create tax deductions where you had none before is the formula to paying less in taxes.

Habit 2: Shift your attitude about audits. Most fear in life comes from lack of knowledge. When you are using legal tax strategies with good records to support them there is no reason to fear an IRS audit. At worst, an audit is a time-consumer you would rather not have in your life. This is a good reason not to want to be called for an audit, but not a reason to fear one. Audits are a hassle, but filing a short form does not protect you from being audited. It'll only waste your money.

There have been some cases of harassment, but over the years, with the millions and millions of returns the agency has processed, these are unusual situations. If this happens to you, the first course of action is to speak to the group manager. If this is to no avail, find out to whom the group manager reports. This is typically a branch chief.

Your best protection is the tax professional who compiled your tax return. A good tax professional has an understanding and a veteran's inside knowledge of how to handle your case. He knows how to talk to the IRS agents so as not to cause additional questions. He understands the time elements the agents have to work under and can use them to your advantage, and save you time by representing you.

If you are involved in an audit now, under the Taxpayer's Bill of Rights you can stop proceedings to bring in a tax professional.

Habit 3: Keep a good paper trail to back up your tax strategies. Question: "What is the IRS looking for?" Answer: "Unsubstantiated deductions."

For travel and entertainment, substantiate your expenditures with receipts that confirm whom you entertained and business relationship to you, when you were with them, where the event took place, what the business purpose was, and how much you spent, with a receipt for anything over $25.

Additionally, keep receipts for interest you pay on money borrowed for investments, medical expenses, charitable contributions, taxes, self-employed business expenses, and miscellaneous deductions. Keep a written record of all deductible expenses under $25. Self-employed persons can now deduct 25 percent of the cost of health insurance for themselves and their families.

Question: "What is the IRS looking for?" Answer: "Unreported income."

Watch that you have good documentation for inheritances, borrowing, repaid loans, bank transfers, successful investments, appreciation of assets, and nontaxable windfalls such as an award of damages in a lawsuit. The Bank Receipts and Bank Statements files appear obvious; again, however, it is important to *be sure to track all deposits.*

To do this, simply make duplicate deposit slips each time you make a deposit: one for you and one for the bank. On your slip write down where the deposit came from: salary, dividend, loan reimbursement, etc.

How important is this? George S. Alberts, former director of the Albany and Brooklyn IRS districts, told *TAX HOTline*, a tax-information newsletter, "All IRS enforcement personnel—auditors, revenue agents, special agents, revenue officers, and estate tax attorneys—are trained to detect possible fraud by taxpayers. The prize they're looking for is substantial unreported income.

Here is an example: You probably have a money market account that has limited checking but a great interest rate. Your checking account needs an infusion; you make the transfer and forget to document it. Two and a half years later you find yourself in an audit with the IRS. They want you to account for all of your deposits for the year in question, which took place some two and a half foggy years ago. And there you are tearing your hair out trying to figure out where that deposit came from.

Tip: There are times when you may need someone more responsive to talk to at the IRS. If there has been a bureaucratic mix-up, if an IRS action against you poses a significant hardship, if your tax refund is missing, or if you've received a notice from the IRS you don't understand, and you can't get anyone at the IRS to explain it to you, you can call the Problem Resolution Office (PRO) at any IRS district office. They will be sure your problem is taken care of. You can get a copy of IRS publication 1320, *Operation Link,* which lists the phone numbers and addresses of all the PROs by calling the IRS toll-free number at 800-829-3676.

Being on top of the tax laws and keeping your tax professional closely informed as to your business and tax strategies will lessen the possibility of any adverse ordeals.

Habit 4: Quit thinking of tax advisors as luxuries. Since your greatest single expense each year is probably your tax bill, find a good tax professional. "Why should I pay a tax professional when I've been taking care of my returns all along?"

With very few exceptions, most people cannot stay on top of all the changes and nuances in the tax laws. You are a professional or specialist in what you do for a living, and in most cases it takes additional education to keep on top of your field. The same goes for good tax professionals; they must attend continuing education classes to stay on top of their field. Do you have time to attend tax classes? If you did, would you grasp the jargon that is used?

If you use the filing system from chapter 13, and keep up on the media's reports on taxes, you can reduce your taxes, reduce your tax professional's bill, and improve the quality of your lifestyle.

The definition of a good tax professional is a person who conscientiously works with you to lower your tax bill. A good tax professional will be concerned about the tax aspects of your investments with regard to your goals, needs, and your tax liability. At your first visit, a good tax professional will look at your past three years' tax returns and determine if he can immediately save you some taxes. Then he will ask questions to get an idea of where you could implement some tax savings strategies.

Interview several tax professionals to get a feeling for how aggressive they are with their interpretation of the rules. Some are intimidated by the tax laws. Get references from friends and ask how much they paid in taxes the previous year.

Habit 5:   Keep in touch with your tax professional. You may be able to deduct part of that vacation.

Call your tax professional any time you are making changes in your life, such as investments, purchase of a new auto, sale of your home, purchase of a second home, divorce, marriage, or any major happenings in your life, including your vacation. By proper planning, you may be able to spend part of your vacation time working or trying to purchase a business and be allowed to deduct part of the cost of the vacation.

Habit 6:   Keep up to date on exactly what lowers your

adjusted gross income (AGI). This includes among others things deductible contributions to an IRA, contributions to 403(b) and 401(k) plans and pension and profit-sharing plans (be sure to take advantage of these), alimony payments, loss from small businesses, deductions from real estate investments, half of your self-employment tax, and premature withdrawal penalties from Certificates of Deposit. Your goal is to reduce your adjusted gross income.

Habit 7: Explore how you can start a small business to take advantage of the deductions it offers. Investigate opportunities you hear about, or consider specializing in a particular aspect of your present career and become a consultant. You can also start figuring out how to turn what you love to do into a small business.

Habit 8: Make tax information priority reading. The more you know, the more money you can save, and the more you can maximize your spendable income and enjoy a better lifestyle. This needn't be a painful experience. With all the creative ways there are to communicate to the nonprofessional about taxes, you could almost consider keeping up your tax education as light reading. Here are two newsletters to help you out:

- *Bottom Line* (1-800-274-5611). This is a neat little newsletter you can whip through in twenty minutes without a dictionary. Each month they have excellent suggestions for tax protection strategies, as well as other money management tactics to which you can easily relate.
- *TAX HOTline* (1-800-288-1051) This is slightly heavier reading but still easy, and you will pick up the most up-to-date strategies, rulings, and experiences in this newsletter. It's worth the money.

Making It Happen

The objective of this chapter was to start you on your way to good tax planning habits, yet not overwhelm you with drudgery.

Your tax planning must be doable or it won't happen. Use tax professionals so you can have time to do what you love to do best, and be sure to keep informed so you can work in tandem with your tax professional to save your money.

As a Result of This Chapter

What strategies did you learn from this chapter?

Accordingly, what action are you going to take today that will be to your advantage?

15

A Tax Shelter Is Not to Be Ignored

Eighty percent of life is just showing up.
—Woody Allen

Your goal is to reduce your adjusted gross income. Your primary goal is to increase your tax-free investment capital. Your company's pension plan, a personal Keogh, and your IRA account are very important to your bottom line. Usually they lower your adjusted gross income on your tax return, and they always allow your money to grow, tax-free. You knew all that, but did you know that your retirement plans add to your self esteem. How?

For one thing, you become a portfolio money manager overnight which instantly moves you out of the couch potato definition. Second, you get the government to work for you as a partner in your investment program when you take advantage of compounding on a tax-free basis. Third, and most importantly, you are doing something for yourself and for your future. There is nothing more satisfying than knowing you are taking control of an aspect of your life.

Since the beginning of this year, we have been waiting for Congress and the White House to pass and sign the 1996 budget. Attached to that yet-to-be-passed piece of legislation are changes in IRA and pension contributions. Jim Sears from the marketing department of Resources Trust Company in Denver, Colorado has provided a list of some of the changes that are of a less technical nature which will impact upon the general public:

Deductible IRA: Increases in deductibility and contributions for both spouses which will be indexed to inflation. Additionally, there would be special circumstances for penalty-free withdrawals which are unavailable now.

American Dream IRA: The bottom line to this idea is that you could put away after-tax dollars in a tax-deferred instrument. After five years you could withdraw your money without penalty for your first home up to $10,000, education expenses, medical expenses, and unemployment problems.

SIMPLE: This is a plan for employers with less than one hundred employees. It would make it simpler and less costly to have a pension plan for their employees. The good news is that every employee can put up to $6,000 away with no discrimination toward highly-paid employees. However, an employer match is required which many owners of small companies balk at.

Medical Savings Account: This would be a trust or custodial account similar to an IRA for individuals with high-deductible (at least $1,500) health plans. Your contributions would be deductible but could not exceed the health plan deductible or $2,000. Earnings would be tax-free and distributions would be tax-free for certain qualified medical expenses.

While waiting for the passage of the legislation, the following list is what you can work from today:

IRA   An Individual Retirement Account into which every working American can contribute up to $2,000 or 100 percent of earned income, (whichever is less) every year. Usually, the amount is fully tax-deductible if you or your spouse are not covered by a retirement plan where you work or if you make less than certain limits.

401(k)   A corporate retirement plan funded through payroll deductions, often called a salary reduction or salary savings plan. These plans provide immediate tax savings, and the contribution limits are generally much higher than for IRAs and can have matching contributions from the employer.

403(b)   A retirement plan similar to a 401(k) plan, but for employees of certain tax-exempt and education organizations.

Profit-sharing or Money Purchase Plans (formerly known as Keogh plans.)   A retirement plan for self-employed individuals with yearly limits of $30,000 (or 15 percent of your salary in a profit-sharing plan and 25 percent in a money purchase plan). This is now identical to most standard corporate profit-sharing or money purchase plans.

SEP-IRA (Simplified Employee Pension Plan)   A plan designed for small businesses and self-employed individuals. An employer can contribute up to $30,000 or 15 percent of salary.

SAR-SEP   A SEP-IRA funded through payroll deductions.

Plans and Strategies

Question: What is the right decision as to which vehicle to use and when?

If your company has a 401(k) plan, put as much as you can into that plan before contributing to an IRA. Why?

You are still allowed to invest in your 401(k) with pretax dollars (you can deduct the dollars you save from your gross income leaving you with fewer dollars on which you have to pay taxes for the year) but you may not be able to deduct your IRA contribution; you are probably able to contribute more to the 401(k) plan than to your IRA; your company might match all or a portion of your 401(k) contributions, an attribute no IRA can provide; and you may be able to borrow against the 401(k) or withdraw some money without penalty, which are two more advantages over IRAs.

The Company Plan

If your company offers any type of retirement plan, get to know it now. Ask your employee benefits department, head of personnel, or employer about this plan. Many employees are intimidated by their employers about this subject because they don't know the right questions to ask. So here are eleven questions with which you can arm yourself:

1. What type of retirement plan do I have? Please explain if it defines the benefit I am to receive when I retire or if it defines the contribution that I and/or my employer make to my plan.

2. Is the contribution fixed or is it contributed on a profit sharing basis? In other words, at the end of the year, if the company makes a profit, will the company contribute to my plan?

3. Am I eligible to receive retirement benefits? If not now, when will I be?

4. How much is my plan worth today?

5. Do I have any choices as to where my money is invested? If not, where is it invested, and what is the projected return on the investments? If I do, what choices do I have, and how many times a year can I move my money from one investment to another?

6. Can I make contributions to the plan to enhance the dollar amount? How much and how often?

7. Can I borrow money from my plan? How much and how often?

8. What are the penalties for early withdrawal?

9. What happens if I am disabled or die?

10. What is the retirement age in the plan, and how will the benefits be paid out? What are my options?

11. A very important question in the event of a merger: If the firm is bought by another company or if the firm closes down, what happens to my pension?

Use That IRA

Today, you have to work 122 days to pay your taxes. That amounts to 47 percent of your work days to pay your tax bill.

When you combine the compounded tax-free earnings of an IRA, Keogh, and pension plans with a tax deduction for every dollar invested, you're capturing back some of those days for your goals.

If you can afford to put additional dollars away after you have contributed to your company retirement plan, or if your company does not have a retirement plan, or you have received a lump-sum distribution from a previous employer, congress has given you a retirement plan called the Individual Retirement Account, better known as the IRA.

This little tax shelter works like this:

Anyone who works for pay can invest up to $2,000 a year in an IRA and can fund the account as late as April fifteenth for the previous year's tax return. A married couple with one working spouse can put away $2,500, while a married couple with two incomes can invest $4,000.

Contributions to an IRA are deductible against your gross income on your tax return if neither you nor your spouse is covered by a corporate pension, tax-deferred savings plan, employer-sponsored annuity, or Keogh plan. The operative word here is "covered." You don't have to be vested in your company's pension plan to be covered by it; as soon as your company starts putting money away for you or lets you contribute to a plan you are covered. Ask your employee benefits department or employer if you are covered if you're not sure. All earnings within the IRA are tax-deferred until withdrawal.

You can also continue to deduct your entire contribution to an IRA even if you or your spouse is covered by a company plan if your adjusted gross income is under $40,000. The same goes for a single person if your income is under $25,000.

There is a partial deduction from your gross income if your combined incomes are between $40,000 and $50,000, or $25,000 and $35,000 for a single person. If your income(s) is above these amounts, there is no write-off, but the earnings will still be tax-deferred.

If you invest in an IRA believing you will be able to deduct it and later in the year you realize the IRA will be nondeductible, you will be allowed to withdraw your money without owing an IRS penalty. On the other hand you may want to take advantage of the tax-deferred savings ability of the IRA and leave your money in the plan. Under this scenario, you will not owe income taxes on the nondeductible contributions upon withdrawing the cash. Only your deductible earnings and contributions will be taxed.

Early withdrawals before age fifty-nine-and-a-half are generally assessed at a 10 percent tax penalty. However, if you take the money out of your IRA in equal installments over your lifetime you will forego this penalty.

If you receive a lump sum payment from the pension plan of your previous employer, or you want to transfer your IRA from one account to another, you have sixty days in which to roll your payout into what is known as an IRA rollover or make your transfer without being penalized.

Is There an Annuity in Your Life?

If you have utilized all your before-tax opportunities for saving your money tax-deferred and have the opportunity to save additional dollars, you may want to look into an annuity. Annuities are tax-favored investment plans to which you contribute after-tax dollars but enable your gains to grow tax-deferred. The tax-deferral advantage offered by annuities makes them similar to IRAs. But there are three notable differences:

1. There are no restrictions imposed by the Internal Revenue Code on the amount you can invest in an annuity.

2. While contributions to IRAs must be from earned income, the money you invest in an annuity can come from any source, such as earnings, the sale of property, or a gift or inheritance.

3. With an annuity you have greater freedom over when you take withdrawals. There's no requirement that you begin withdrawals at age seventy and a half.

However, as with IRAs, the benefit of tax-deferral comes with a hitch. The government applies a 10 percent tax penalty on withdrawals of earnings before age fifty-nine and a half, in addition to ordinary income taxes. Generally, annuities make sense for investors who are in the 28 percent or above federal tax bracket, and who can hold the annuities for ten years or longer.

This is because it could take that long for the advantage of tax-deferral to offset the cost of the insurance and administrative charges that commonly total about 1.3 percent of assets per year. These are used to pay for distribution costs and for the death benefit guarantee. The guarantee is backed by the insurance company, so it makes sense that you look for insurance companies that are rated at or near the top by independent services like A.M. Best, Moody's and Standard & Poor's. Your financial planner (refer to appendix C for information about financial planners) or securities dealer can supply these ratings.

Additionally, while most annuities have no up-front sales charge, they typically carry a surrender charge on withdrawals in early years.

Tip: Some annuity contracts let you withdraw up to 10 percent of your investment each year without any surrender charge. And neither the surrender charge nor the 10 percent federal tax penalty applies if you begin taking money in substantially equal amounts spread over your life expectancy. Always ask, and ask again, about the charges, fees, and expenses.

Annuities come in two types:

Fixed Annuities—Fixed annuities resemble tax-deferred bank certificates of deposit. You get a promised interest rate the insurer sets for a specific period, usually one year, after which the rate is reset.

Variable Annuities—With variable annuities, you direct your money among a variety of options that resemble tax-deferred mutual funds. Your return depends on the results achieved by the funds you've selected and you assume the risk. On the other hand, if you select an insurance company that has teamed up with one of the leading mutual fund managers, you are in a position to earn potentially higher rewards than in fixed annuities. Some variable annuities offer several different mutual fund company managers to choose from and guarantee your original investment plus some interest to your beneficiaries. This last feature gives some peace of mind to those that worry that the stock market might crash and lose their money.

Another favorable point is that ordinarily, exchanges between mutual funds, even within the same family, are considered sales, and any gains are fully taxable; not so under the variable annuity's tax-shelter umbrella.

To round out the picture, annuities have two phases over their lifetime: an asset-building or accumulation period during which your money grows, tax-deferred, and a payout period during which you either withdraw your cash in a lump sum, make withdrawals as needed, or annuitize the contract, meaning you take a stream of monthly payments guaranteed to last for the rest of your life. Remember, earnings are taxed when withdrawn regardless of when or the payout option.

When considering an annuity, remember your goals. Annuities are not all-purpose tax shelters, nor are they places to invest money you may need soon. Keep your rainy day funds, the money you've earmarked to take a vacation, and moneys saved for buying a home elsewhere. Annuities work best for funding retirement long-term.

As a Result of This Chapter

What are the biggest changes you can implement from reading this chapter?

What one thing in this chapter caught your attention that you are going to act on today?

16

Insure What?

The real purpose of books is to trap the mind into doing its own thinking.
                                        —Christopher Morley

Helping you pay yourself first is one of the objectives of this book. When reviewing my clients' use of their money, 98 percent of the time I find a misuse of dollars in insurance costs. Usually it is because they are buying too much coverage in one area and not enough in another area, particularly in the area of liability. The following chapter is a guideline to help you review your insurance and become adept at asking competent questions of your insurance professionals. Remember: The big print giveth and the small print taketh away.

Homeowners' Insurance

Accidents happen. They can happen to you. So can disasters. While writing my first book, my close friends Rod and Teri Hensley lost their home and its entire contents in a firestorm which for two days charred the hills above Oakland, California. At least twenty-four people were killed and more than 2,800 homes were destroyed. The fire was so swift that cars were igniting as people tried to get away in them to save their lives.

75

If you're like most people, you think such disasters could never happen to you. Or, if a tragedy of this magnitude were to occur, you might think that there was nothing you could have done to prepare for it. You can't stop these quirks of fate, but you can protect yourself against financial devastation.

Here's how you can get the most for your dollar while protecting yourself against disaster.

Features to Look For

The best policies all share two principal features:

1. They provide *open perils* coverage. This means you are insured against damage from any risk *except those that are specifically excluded,* such as earthquake, flood, war, and nuclear accident. An open perils policy is usually referred to as Homeowners' 3, and either that name or its abbreviation, HO-3, should appear on the first page of your policy. Homeowners' (HO) insurance generally comes in three grades, with HO-1 being the most basic and H0-3 the most comprehensive. HO-1, for example, does not cover burst pipes, but H0-2 and H0-3 do. You want HO-3 for best coverage. If you have an unusually expensive or custom-built home, compare the increased benefits, albeit higher premiums, of an HO-5. (HO-4 policies cover apartment dwellers and other renters. HO-6 policies cover condominium and co-op owners.)

2. They contain a *replacement cost* clause that obligates the insurer to pay the full cost of repairing or replacing your home up to the dollar limit of your policy. Having the right amount of replacement coverage is critical. Make sure the replacement coverage is indexed to inflation with an inflation guard endorsement.

Most policies cover the contents of the house for 50 percent to 75 percent of the amount for which the house is insured. So if your house is insured for $100,000, the contents are insured for $50,000 to $75,000. You can beef up your contents coverage by paying an additional premium for a Scheduled Property endorsement. Make sure you have replacement-cost coverage for your contents in writing (other types subtract for depreciation); and an inventory of what you own and what each item is worth. Keep this inventory list in some other location. Videotapes or snapshots will help establish that you did, in fact, possess the contents you are claiming were lost or destroyed.

Consider getting *umbrella* coverage if your personal assets are worth more than the liability limits on your insurance. Your liability coverage doesn't protect you from being sued for libel, wrongful eviction, discrimination, or invasion of privacy. You could be sued for an amount equal to the value of your assets and be forced to come up with the cash if you lose the case.

Four Ways to Save

1. Check whether discounts are offered if you have protective devices such as smoke alarms, deadbolt locks, and fire extinguishers.

2. Self insure by taking the largest deductible you can afford. Raise the deductible to $500 or more. As your assets and income increase, increase your deductible accordingly.

3. Shop your coverage. Know exactly what you want and shop for the lowest rates.

4. If you want your mortgage paid off if you should die don't buy mortgage life insurance. Buy annually renewable term life insurance; it's cheaper.

Auto Insurance

Standards and state-set minimums vary widely depending, for example, on whether you live in a no-fault state. Here are some basics to protect you financially.

Features to Look For

Your minimum liability coverage, which protects you when your car harms someone or something else, should be $100,000 per injured person, $300,000 total per accident, and $50,000 for property damage. This part of your auto insurance covers any legal costs and any legal liability.

Tip: Carry enough bodily injury liability insurance to cover your net assets plus attorneys' fees. For a relatively small amount, $100 to $200 a year, you can buy a $1,000,000 worth of protection against a huge liability lawsuit. The above mentioned umbrella liability policy picks up where the liability portions of auto and homeowners' policies leave off. You're an especially good candidate for this type of suit if you have substantial assets or the potential for strong future earnings.

Medical payments coverage (for injuries to people in your car regardless of liability) might overlap your own health care coverage but not your passengers'. It's worth it. Typically, medical payments coverage is limited to $1,000 or $5,000 per person.

Collision and comprehensive coverage pays for damage to your car. Comprehensive pays for damage by fire, theft, or anything but collision. Collision pays for damage to your car by collision with another car or object.

If you take the time to do some calculating, you may be able to do without uninsured motorist coverage, which pays for injuries to you or your passengers caused by hit-and-run, uninsured, or underinsured drivers. Look at your health and collision coverage; it may already cover you. If you live in a strong no-fault state, you may be covered. Some states, though, require you to carry uninsured motorist coverage. If you do need it, consider $100,000 per injured individual and $300,000 total per accident.

Personal-injury protection (PIP) is required in states with no-fault insurance. PIP covers your medical bills as well as some portion of wages lost if you are disabled in an accident, and picks up your damages even if someone else caused the accident. One way you can save on PIP is if your health plan states it is the primary payer for accident-related medical bills. You could cut your costs by as much as 40 percent.

Six Ways to Save

1. Shop for the lowest rate. Don't assume all insurance companies charge identical premiums. You may be able to save as much as $400 to $500 annually by comparison shopping.

2. Insure all household cars with the same company; you can save between 15 percent and 25 percent by consolidating your car insurance with the same company.

3. Consider doing without comprehensive and collision insurance if your car's value has dropped below $1,500. Insurers reimburse you for the amount the car is worth at the time of the accident. No matter how much insurance you own, an insurance company will never pay more than the book value. If you decide to keep collision and comprehensive, take the highest deductible you can afford.

4. Raise deductibles as high as $500 to $1000.

5. Never file an insurance claim for under $500. The insurance company will bump your premium next year, or worse yet, cancel your policy.

6. Check discounts that may be available in the 5 percent to 20 percent range, including those for safe drivers, nonsmokers, honor-roll students, graduates of driver's ed courses, completing defensive-driving courses, no accidents in three years, female-driver and/or senior-citizen discounts, no moving violations in three years, antitheft devices, low annual mileage, automatic seat belts, air bag, and antilock brakes, and combined auto and homeowners' coverage with the same company.

Health Insurance

Features to Look For

To get the best health coverage for your dollar, here, from a Bureau of Labor Statistics survey of employers, are guidelines for better-than-average coverage for traditional care:

1. doctor visits both in and out of hospital, 80 percent covered

2. semiprivate hospital room, 100 percent for 120-plus days

3. surgical fees, 100 percent covered

4. lab fees and X rays, 80 percent covered

5. nursing, 80 percent covered

6. mental health and substance abuse treatment, 100 percent of inpatient services up to thirty days and limited outpatient therapy covered

7. dental injuries, 80 percent covered

8. miscellaneous dental care, 50 percent to 100 percent covered, with a $2,000 annual limit

Six Ways to Save

When weighing health insurance options, the following precautions are necessary when purchasing insurance for health care and reviewing your contract:

1. Focus on the four principal elements of any policy, which are:

The maximum lifetime payment. Think in terms of a catastrophic misfortune and look for how much in your lifetime the company will pay, regardless of how exorbitant your medical bills may become. You want the highest maximum lifetime benefit.

The co-insurance provision is the percentage of the bill you pay, and this will vary. If you have an individual policy, keep your premium down by choosing at least a 20 percent out-of-pocket provision.

The stop-loss limit is the amount at which the company starts paying 100 percent of all eligible covered expenses. You pay a total out-of-pocket limit within a certain period, which is usually a year. After that amount the insurer picks up 100 percent of your expenses. The higher the stop-loss breakpoint, the lower the premiums.

The deductible should be as high as your short-term savings and emergency fund will allow you to self-insure. The more of the costs you can pick up yourself, the lower your premiums will be.

2. Evaluate if your family may be more prone to accidents and health problems than the average family. Determine if you would be dollars ahead with higher coverage even though your premiums are higher.

3. Medical insurance should be purchased only from state-licensed carriers. Stay away from mail order or TV insurance offers, even if they come with your credit card statement. The insurance is high and most likely contains limited benefits you won't understand until it's too late.

4. Examine the policy meticulously before you buy it. If the agent doesn't provide you with a copy of the policy, move on to · other agents that will. Then, after the insurance company has all your information, check for any conditions that may have been imposed on the contract as a result of this information.

5. When it comes to your insurance, think of your family as another business you are running. Understand the specific coverage you need, and shop for it.

6. Be sure to keep watch over the two areas most people overlook.

Employees with employee medical benefits often assume every situation is covered. Don't assume. Get your employee benefit book out and go through it carefully. Understand situations for which you are covered and, more importantly, those for which you are not covered. If you're a new employee, does your medical coverage start immediately?

You looked into all the medical and hospital costs when you acquired your insurance, and you assume you're still adequately covered. Again, don't assume. Policies two years or older can be out of touch with current costs and may need updating or supplementing. Some policies contain riders that permit you to increase your limits at such times.

More and more companies are arranging for partially self-funded medical insurance plans. These plans can lower employee and employer costs. Be sure to ask your employer if they have looked into them.

For prepaid plans, such as HMOs, you want to be aware that you usually are expected to use their staff doctors. This type of coverage may be attractive if you want first-dollar coverage. Most other medical services are fully covered, although mental health care is usually limited to thirty to sixty inpatient days and twenty to thirty days of outpatient therapy at $20 per visit. Unlike other insurance plans, HMOs typically have no deductibles or maximum lifetime benefits and pay a higher percentage of the cost of hospital stays and surgery. Be sure to look into this type of coverage as a possible alternative to your needs.

Disability Insurance

Features to Look For

Like most people, you probably think that worker's compensation and Social Security disability insurance will cover you if you can't work for a period of time. But that coverage usually isn't adequate; and if you were injured or become sick away from your job, worker's compensation won't pay at all. As for help from Social Security, you must wait six months before your Social Security disability checks start to arrive. Plus you won't get any Social Security disability benefits at all unless you can prove that you will not be able to engage in substantial, gainful activity for more than a year or that your disability will result in death.

When looking at disability policies, you will find that, generally, insurers will cover up to 60 to 65 percent of your gross salary. If you are self-employed, shoot for 70 percent of after-tax income so that the policy will help reimburse the overhead costs of your business. Here are other important features:

Be sure your policy is noncancelable and guaranteed renewable with benefits to age sixty-five, or better yet, for life, if you can afford it.

Many policies stop payments the day you return to work even if you can only work part time. Ask for a policy that has residual benefits, which are for people who can only work part time and earn less than 80 percent of their salary. This policy will pay benefits in proportion to lost income while the person works part time.

There are a variety of definitions for "disability." You want the most liberal available to you, which would state your "inability to perform one or more of your primary duties of your present occupation."

Two Ways to Save

1. Use the same approach that works for homeowners' and auto coverage; opt for the longer elimination period (90 to 180 days). This decreases your premium substantially.

2. Add a Social Security integration rider, which, if you qualify, reduces your regular disability income check by exactly the amount the government provides you. If you do not qualify for this Social Security supplement, you're still paid the promised amount by the insurance company; but, by agreeing to seek Social Security if you are disabled, you may decrease your policy premium further.

If you're employed, you may be covered by a disability policy, but they are usually limited in what they offer. Look over what your employer's policy covers; you may want to add a supplemental policy.

Life Insurance

Features to Look For

If you have dependents that depend on you for their support, you need life insurance. Buy a large enough life insurance benefit that, if invested at 8 percent per year, will provide 75 percent of your current family income.

When you buy annual renewable term life insurance you are buying pure life insurance; however, each year your cost for the insurance goes up. When you're younger, this insurance is by far the cheapest; but, as you get older, the costs become quite high. You may feel you only need life insurance for a short term need. Be sure your policy is renewable regardless of changes in your health. This prevents the insurance company from canceling your policy at the end of any year. If your insurance company reserves the right to raise rates under certain circumstances, be sure you know in advance the maximum rate you can be charged.

The main advantage of the term policy is that you can get substantial coverage for much less money than you can with the whole life policy. During times in life when money is very tight, this is your best buy.

Whole life insurance is considered permanent because the amount of cash you pay each year does not change. Once you have the insurance, you never have to qualify for it again. The insurance company picks up the increase from the money you already paid in excess premiums during your younger years and which has accumulated in an account called cash value. This account has been earning interest. Even though your out-of-pocket cost may not change, the premium always does go up.

You probably are questioning why anyone would buy anything but term life insurance. Some people buy whole life products because they like the "forced savings" function of it. The savings comes from paying excess premiums at an early age. If this is your reasoning, as a financial planner, I would rather see you buy term and invest the difference through an automatic savings withdrawal plan from your checking account into a mutual fund.

On the other hand, there are plenty of reasons for longer-lived baby-boomers to take a look at whole life. Until the mid eighties, whole-life was not much of a buy. It often cost ten times as much as term insurance for someone in his mid-thirties, and the savings portion of the policy earned a paltry 2 to 6 percent annual return. A disciplined investor could have bought term for much less money and put the savings in an investment with a far better return.

But whole life has become more respectable over the past several years. Many insurers now invest the savings portion of policies to earn around 8 percent a year, which is tax-deferred until the money is withdrawn. Under current tax law, if you borrow against the cash value of the policy there are no taxes because it is money you have deposited after paying taxes on it originally. Since the Tax Reform Act of the mid eighties, this appeal has increased substantially.

Another factor to consider for whole life insurance is the new policies which offer you the option to withdraw against the death benefit (the amount of money for which you are insured) in the event you need the money for long term care. Different companies have different limits and procedures to determine how much and when you can withdraw your money if you need it this way. Shop around and compare.

Four Ways to Save

1. If you are single and have no dependents you don't need life insurance unless you want to protect your assets against taxes for your heirs. No one is going to miss your income in the event of your death.

2. Never buy life insurance on children. Insurance is needed only by those who are providing an income for dependents or protecting assets from taxes for their heirs. If you want to do something for your children's future, invest the money in a mutual fund.

3. If you have decided whole life is for you, look for policies that guarantee to pass through the full and complete net investment earnings on life insurance contracts for the life of the contract; guarantee fixed expense for the life of the contract; and guarantee to pass through the lowest mortality charges available to the company from its reinsurers for the life of the contract.

4. If you can't get an 8 percent return, ask your agent about variable life insurance. Variable life insurance gives you the opportunity to invest your cash values in stock and bond positions.

You Can Give Yourself a Raise

Give yourself a raise by understanding the primary principal for buying insurance, which is: Get the broadest possible coverage you can, but don't pay to insure a loss you could afford to absorb yourself. Your goal here is to self insure by having an emergency cash reserve equal to between three and six months of your family's typical expenses. This reserve will allow you to lower your premiums by taking higher deductibles.

Give yourself another raise by not buying unnecessary insurance. Watch out for the following:

- Credit life and disability insurance are voluntary and expensive. When you're in your thirties and forties, you can usually get the same coverage for less money by buying term life insurance or disability insurance from an insurance agent.
- Flight insurance and cancer insurance are too limited to be economical.
- When asked to sign a collision-damage waiver before renting a car, check your own auto insurance. Most comprehensive policies cover a rented car's full value in case of theft, vandalism, or accident, and many pay for loss of use. Most Visa and MasterCard gold cards and American Express give full coverage for accidents, vandalism, theft, and loss of use when you use them to rent a car.
- While you're checking the comprehensive coverage of your auto insurance, check your homeowners' or tenants' policy for stolen personal property coverage, even when it's stolen from a rental car. You're most likely covered; so if you are, save some more money and don't pay for the personal

effects coverage (PEC) when you're renting a car.
- When asked to purchase supplemental liability insurance (SLI) at the rental car counter, if you own a car, you probably already have sufficient liability insurance. If you don't, buy the extra coverage.
- One more place you can save at the car rental counter is the personal accident insurance (PAI). If you already have health and life insurance pass up this extra.

You can cut your premiums if you are diligent about understanding how much coverage you really need. Pick up the phone and do some comparison shopping. Think of your personal finances as a business.

Sizing Up Your Insurer

Until recently, the notion of the insurance industry being in trouble would have been unthinkable. The staid whole-life policies showed steady but unspectacular returns. During the 1980s, mutual funds and other competitors emerged with returns that put whole life insurance to shame, so insurers began offering a host of new products that promised amazing performances—in some cases, too amazing.

The life insurance industry is extremely concerned about the consumer's view of the industry as a whole. Most people have little to worry about the collapse of the industry; but, don't let that fact drop your guard.

What can you do?

- Watch the media for any bad news about your company's performance.
- Compare your insurance company's ratings by several major ratings agencies. The higher the grades, and the more the different agencies agree, the better.
- Contact the company directly; ask questions about the company's investment practices and portfolio.
- Get in touch with your state insurance department, and ask

about the last time your company was examined. Request a copy of the examination report.

- If you're considering a transfer to another insurance company, ask your insurer or agent what paperwork you'll need to complete the transaction, and what penalties you may incur. Be sure to ask about tax liabilities, too. You may want to consider an alternative, such as borrowing against your current policy. In some cases, moving your policy to another company might be wise. Even though it may cost money to do so, it's better than waking up one morning to read about your insurer in the business pages.

Take another look at your insurance coverage whenever you have a major change in your economic status, like a higher-paying job, a new home purchase, the birth of a child, retirement, or divorce.

As a Result of This Chapter

What major changes do you plan to make to enhance your ability to accumulate money more effortlessly?

17

So You Have Children

It goes without saying that you should never have more children than you have car windows.

—Erma Bombeck

During my daughter's senior year in high school, my daughter and I went to an orientation for the California University system. By the time we left I felt that an applicant had to walk on water and sit on the right-hand side of You-Know-Who in order to get accepted. But that didn't deter my daughter, Trish, for a second. She went for it and got accepted to the college of her choice, which was UCLA.

Tell your child to go for it. Always try for the dream. Worst case: she's rejected, but she'll learn from the experience. She'll learn about her feelings as she goes through the process; she'll learn how much competing for "the big one" affects her emotionally, and she can use that experience when she's going for "the big one" in the business world.

Does college pay? They do if you're a good open field runner.

—Will Rogers

If your child wants to attend one of the Ivy League schools, but is not a great scholar, or has no exceptional talents (such as

89

State Volleyball Champion or Artist of the Year), it is best that she have a couple of alternative schools in mind. The kid that is a well-rounded student who gets good grades, plays sports, edits the school newspaper, and has a lot of outside interests falls into the largest group swamping the prestige colleges. Today, these colleges are looking for a well-rounded freshman class of unusually exceptional people rather than a class full of well-rounded individuals. But if acceptance to one of the Ivies has always been your child's dream, by all means, urge her to go for it. Your child could be exceptional regular folk.

Mastering the Admissions Process

Trish was accepted to UCLA because she focused on the application essay. Concentrating on this essay is most important, because it is the area which distinguishes one student from another. The key is for the student to focus on why she would be an asset to the institution; how well she performs when operating at or near the peak of her abilities; her accomplishments, including specific examples of successful performance and the results produced whenever possible; and appealing aspects of her personality, character, or attitudes.

But be sure your child writes her own essay, because according to Richard Moll, author of *Playing the Private College Admissions Games* and *The Ivies* (Penguin Books), it comes over more sincerely than a professionally packaged essay or even one polished by Mom or Dad.

If a high score on the SATs (Scholastic Aptitude Test) or the ACTs (American College Testing Assessment) is important for your child to get into the college of her choice, a coaching school and/or books that prepare her for the exams are worth the time and money invested. Taking a preparation course familiarizes her with the instructions, types of questions, and time pressures she will experience on the test day. Your child will learn how to pace herself as well as little tricks for making informed guesses and taking short cuts. Two books worth considering are *How to Prepare for College Board Achievement Tests,* published by Barron's, and another called *10 SATs,* published by the College Board.

Two more points to be aware of are:

- Be sure to provide the recommendations the college requests, which are usually school-related. Extra recommendations from friends are unnecessary and may seem over zealous.
- Be sure your child goes for the campus interview. Usually teenagers make a better impression in person than on paper. If an interview is not offered, have your child find a hometown alumnus and ask him to meet with your child; then ask him to make an official report to the institution. You don't know anyone from the college your child is interested in? A few phone calls to your friends and business acquaintances will usually produce one.

Understanding College Costs

The earlier you start a college fund for your child, the easier it is on your budget because that good old rule of compounding helps accumulate the money you'll need. Your portfolio strategy can afford to be aggressive in the first fourteen years of your child's life. An easy way to start is with growth mutual funds which invest in stocks of established companies with the potential for long-term capital appreciation; then hold them for at least a decade. Starting around her fourteenth birthday, gradually move to a more mixed portfolio of fixed-income investments such as certificates of deposit and money funds so that you will have ready money by the time it is needed for her tuition.

The following table demonstrates how much you'd have to invest, either in a lump sum or monthly, to meet the projected cost of a public or private college, assuming your money compounds at a rate of 8 percent a year.

Your, Child's Age	Years Until College	What You Need to Invest in a Lump Sum Today		What You Need to Invest Monthly	
		Public College	*Private College*	*Public College*	*Private College*
Newborn	18	$18,816	$39,893	$ 157	$ 332
1	17	19,171	40,645	164	348
2	16	19,533	41,412	173	368
3	15	19,902	42,194	182	387
4	14	20,277	42,990	193	410
5	13	20,660	43,797	206	436
6	12	21,049	44,627	220	467
7	11	21,447	45,469	237	503
8	10	21,851	46,327	258	547
9	9	22,264	47,209	283	599
10	8	22,684	48,092	314	665
11	7	23,111	48,999	353	749
12	6	23,548	49,924	406	861
13	5	23,992	50,866	480	1,017
14	4	24,445	51,825	590	1,251
15	3	24,906	52,803	774	1,641
16	2	25,376	53,800	1,141	2,420
17	1	25,855	54,815	2,243	4,755

Four-year costs, including tuition, fees, room and board, books, and transportation, are based on the 1989 College Board Annual Survey of Colleges. The 1989 costs were $27,923 for public and $59,200 for private colleges and have been projected based on an assumed 6% annual increase in college expenses.

Any high school student with at least a B average and College Board scores above the national norm is in the running for an academic scholarship. Don't let preconceived financial ideas stop your child from applying to the college of her choice. By all means, encourage her to apply to that prestigious university you think you can't afford.

Sometimes the most expensive schools give the most generous scholarships. And, don't think your family doesn't qualify for financial aid just because you make $120,000 a year. There are about thirty variables which are taken into account when considering a case, which include family size, age of the older parent, number of children in college, graduate school, or a high-tuition private secondary school at the same time, and unusual medical expenses.

Before your child's junior year in high school, it's most important that you be aware of the form in which your assets are held. Here are some important aspects to be alert to:

If you are going to sell securities you own to pay for your child's education, sell them and take the capital gains before December 31 of her junior year of high school. Capital gains are considered income and reduce your eligibility for assistance.

Don't list assets that you don't have access to such as funds in IRAs or pension accounts.

Don't take money out of pension programs or IRAs for college expenses. You will have to pay taxes on that money and if you don't withdraw the money in equal amounts each year for either the next five years or until you reach fifty-nine and a half, whichever comes later, you will be penalized on the money. Additionally, it will increase the income that the financial aid formulas take into account in figuring eligibility for aid. If you have to use retirement moneys, it would be better to borrow the money while the child is in school and then pay back the loan by taking assets out of pension accounts after the child graduates.

The idea of encouraging your child to earn and save by holding a part-time job during high school is no doubt wonderful for the child's character, but the money earned will reduce the child's eligibility for aid. Up to 70 percent of the child's income in the year prior to application is considered available to meet college expenses.

Many tax advisors counsel their clients to put assets in a child's name once she reaches thirteen so that income will be taxed at the child's tax rate. This tactic can cause the loss of financial aid because if a child entering college has substantial assets in her own name, the school will require that the child spend a large portion of those assets before becoming eligible for tuition assistance. Thousands of dollars of tuition aid may be lost.

Don't forget to list medical insurance premiums automatically deducted from your paychecks.

To apply for financial aid you will need to fill out a financial need analysis form called the *Financial Aid Form (FAF)* or the *Family Financial Statement (FFS)* which your child can pick up from her high school guidance counselor. It records your family size, income, assets, household expenses, and other information. The information then is analyzed in order to arrive at a figure known as your family contribution. The catalogs of the schools your child is applying to will state what document is required.

Tip: Be sure to send this form in, certified mail, return receipt requested, as soon as possible after January 1 of the year your child will enter college, even if it means you can only estimate your taxes.

Be sure to get the financial aid application filed by the deadlines set by the colleges. Don't wait until your child is accepted, as financial aid is granted on a first-come first-served basis, and the amount of money available at any particular school is limited. You may be as qualified as the family whose application was considered just ahead of yours, but they might get the last dollar.

Regarding Prepay Programs

Prepay programs offered by universities to frightened parents concerned about rising tuition costs have several considerations. Prepay programs, in principle, work this way: You pay a lump sum in the early years of your child's life and, upon her graduation from high school, your child is guaranteed up to four years of tuition with no additional cost. Things to be evaluated are:

- The IRS has ruled that the difference between your original payment and the value of the future tuition will be taxable to your child as income during her college years.
- You're liable for federal gift tax on whatever amount you put into the plan, since the IRS states that the payment of money is a gift from which the recipient will benefit in the future and it does not represent "present interest" in the money given and, therefore, does not qualify for the $10,000 ($20,000 if both of you gift) exclusion. You can file Form 709, which will allow you to subtract the amount from the $192,800 tax credit allowed against your estate when you die.
- Your child may not want to attend college at all or go to the college of your choice, or may not be accepted by the college.
- Another consideration is the disadvantage of tying up a large amount of your money, leaving it unavailable to work for you in other areas.

Other Ways to Crack the Nut

Whole books are written, and consulting careers developed, to help your child get into and finance her college years. For $7.95 (postage and handling included), *U.S. News and World Report* will send you *America's Best Colleges* (1-800-234-7323). The objective of this book is to help you to pick the right school and finance your child's education. It even includes a computer program that will automatically pick the top ten schools best suited to your child's situation.

For a free booklet on financial aid information for grants, loans, and work-study from the U.S. Department of Education, write to Consumer Information Center, Dept. 506X, Pueblo, Colorado 81009.

An excellent source for finding out about scholarships is Oreon Keeslar's *Financial Aids for Higher Education,* published by William C. Brown. Of course, high school guidance counselors and college admissions officers are also very helpful in this area.

Ask and look into specialized cash awards. For instance, for the artistically inclined, there is an opportunity to compete for awards of up to $3,000 through the National Foundation for Advancement in the Arts. (1-305-573-0490 or write to NFAA, P.O. Box 1305, Miami, Florida).

Other alternatives are:

If graduating from a high-priced school is important to your child and the finances aren't there, have her enroll in a community college, study hard to demonstrate an outstanding academic performance, and then switch to the prestige school and pick up the diploma for one-half to two-thirds of what it would otherwise have cost.

Look into the Reserve Officers Training Corps scholarships sponsored by the U.S. Army, Navy, and Air Force. In exchange for a minimum of eight years of service after graduation on active duty or in the Reserves, or a combination of the two, they will pay full tuition for two to four years plus other benefits such as books, lab fees, and a $100 monthly allowance.

If that looks good, look what the Army National Guard will do for the pledge of a six year hitch of weekends and some summer weeks: Aid up to $9,000 of federal loan forgiveness and a monthly allowance up to $140.

There is also a G.I. Bill worth looking into if she enlists before she enrolls in college and sets aside $1,200 from her Army pay for tuition. After a two-year tour of duty, up to $9,000 is available from the G.I. bill and $8,000 from the Army College Fund if she has served in certain special jobs. Additionally, she can apply for financial aid as a vet which classifies her as an independent student. Aid eligibility is then based on the student's income and assets rather than the parents'. Psychologically, this approach is good because most often a student straight out of high school hasn't a clue as to her major. Joining the Armed Services gives a person time to get to know herself better as well as time to develop some good disciplines.

The Point Is—

In your child's freshman year of high school, start getting a grasp of what it will take on your part and her part to get into college. Too many parents make the mistake of shielding their children from understanding the connection of family economics to their choices of colleges. They tell their child to try to get into the best school that the child possibly can and say, "We'll find a way to pay for it." For a more fruitful college career, sit down with your child and the two of you write out the sacrifices you'll have to make for her education; what she expects from a college education; and what sacrifices she'll need to make. Also, don't hesitate to point out to your child your other financial responsibilities such as additional college educations that are coming up for her brothers or sisters, college or MBA schooling for yourself, or, in some cases, expenses for caring for elderly parents, which leads us right into the next chapter.

As a Result of This Chapter

What action will you take today to create a better understanding in your family of any upcoming college careers?

18

The Mamas and the Papas

It is easier to rule a kingdom than to regulate a family.
—Japanese proverb

"I never expected that when I was a grandparent I'd have to look after my parents," exclaimed Cathy Diehl during a workshop. In recent years the boomer generation is finding itself in a new financial squeeze: increasing economic responsibility, not only for themselves and for their children, but also for their aging parents. For some in this generation, the title of the "Sandwich Generation" seems most appropriate.

Caring for a needy, aging relative has never been so prolonged, nor as common as it will be for the aging boomer. In 1900 there were 13.6 adults between eighteen and sixty-four for each person sixty-five or over. Today the ratio has dropped to 4.8 to 1. In 1900 the average life expectancy was about forty-seven years.

You and Your Parents

It is not only the financially needy that need help. Your parents may be financially independent but have limited money management skills or lack the patience to learn them. Money and mortality are usually very sensitive subjects with aging folks. But it is important that they have the help they need. Take some time to organize your approach to this matter. A possible way to start would be to:

Ask them for the telephone numbers and addresses of people close to them, people that would be of help in case of an emergency. This would include their close neighbors or nearby friends, doctors, dentist, and pharmacist. You may also want to locate the telephone numbers of the police and paramedics.

Then, ask your parents if they feel secure about their finances and their financial future. If they appear confused invite them to compile a list of what they own and what they owe, and what it costs them to live. Tell them you will be glad to help them or you will call on their accountant or bookkeeper to guide them.

If things are still going well, advise them to make a record of whether their assets are held in joint tenancy, tenancy in common, community property, or separately. Suggest that they have a lawyer or financial planner who specializes in estate planning evaluate whether their forms of ownership are advantageous for estate planning purposes. Offer to go with them if this would make them more comfortable.

Remind them that if their wills are older than the 1981 tax law, or if they have moved to another state since their wills were written, these documents should be reviewed by a lawyer. At the same time, it would be advisable for them to look into a living trust as a tool for their estate planning. One important feature of a living trust is if one of your parents should become unable to make financial decisions, an alternate trustee, such as the spouse or possibly yourself, would take over the management of the assets without any hassle.

Talk to your parents about a durable power of attorney. If one or both of your parents is unable to manage their decisions due to senility, illness, or accident, you and/or the other parent will need a durable power of attorney agreement. A power of attorney cannot be executed by an incapable person; therefore, it should be done as part of a routine estate plan. This is an inexpensive way to ensure that people whom your parents trust will manage their affairs when they cannot rather than having to go through the hassle of a court-appointed guardian or conservator.

Also, have a look at the advisability of a living will. This document specifically directs those in charge of their care to terminate treatment under hopeless and terminal circumstances, and if they are being kept alive only by artificial means. In most states, the living will is a separate form created by statute.

If they do not have this type of document, the presumption is that they want treatment to continue. In the absence of a living will, medical treatment will be prolonged unless a lawsuit is brought by family members to stop such treatment. It is far less expensive and emotionally taxing to make their wishes known while they still have the capacity to do so. By the way, this is something all of us need to look into; not just the elderly.

Make sure your parents are getting the benefits they are entitled to by checking that their registrations for Medicare, Social Security, and other programs are in order. Many people don't bother to fill out the complicated Medicare paperwork and miss out on reimbursements.

Help determine, or have a financial planner help them determine whether their income is sufficient for their retirement needs and that their money is invested in the best vehicles for them. Make sure they have a good balance of income to growth investments. In this day of longer lives, keeping part of their money in a growth position is important to maintain their income against inflation. The standard is 60 percent in growth stocks or mutual funds and 40 percent in income-producing investments such as money market accounts, certificates of deposit, Treasury bonds, bills or notes, corporate bonds rated AAA or AA, and municipal bonds.

If your parents' tax rate is higher than 28 percent, tax-exempt money market funds, bonds, and unit trusts may be the answer for them.

For those of you who like to do a little of your own calculating use the following formulas to compute and compare their after-tax yields:

When you know the taxable yield: If their tax rate is 28 percent and the yield on a taxable money fund is 7.64 percent, a tax-free fund *yielding more than* 5.5 percent will pay a higher net return.

Formula:

Tax-Free Yield = Taxable Yield × (1 − Tax Rate)

Example:

Tax-Free Yield = .0764 × (1 − .28) = .055 or 5.5%

When you know the tax-free yield: If their tax rate is 33 percent and the yield on a tax-free fund is 4 percent, a taxable money fund *yielding more than* 5.97 percent will pay them a higher return.

Formula:

$$\text{Taxable Yield} = \frac{\text{Tax-Free Yield}}{1 - \text{Tax Rate}}$$

Example:

$$\text{Taxable Yield} = \frac{.04}{1 - .33} = .0597 \text{ or } 5.97\%$$

Have your parents talk to a good tax accountant to bring them up to date on what tax breaks they should watch out for, such as an additional exemption on their federal income taxes, or breaks on city and state income and property taxes if applicable. Don't forget that people over fifty-five who sell their residence are eligible for a one-time capital gains exclusion of up to $125,000.

Your Parents' Medical Care

When your parents qualify for Medicare, they will also need supplementary health insurance that pays the deductible and the percentage of doctor and hospital bills not reimbursed by Medicare. One supplemental policy placed through a qualified agent is enough.

Nursing home costs are not covered by Medicare or private health insurance. Your parents' odds of going into a nursing home for more than short periods of time are fairly slim, about an 8 percent chance for women, and 5 percent chance for men. Unless frailty or Alzheimer's disease runs in your family, they don't have to rush into nursing home insurance.

If there is a concern about nursing home costs, the Federal Government's Medicaid program can help with the cost of care for people who financially qualify. Judy Copeland, an elder law attorney in San Diego, tells me that, "for a couple where one spouse only is in a nursing home, the qualification guidelines are fairly generous, so do not assume your parents would be ineligible.

" There is a lot of hysteria surrounding the cost of long-term care and some elderly people are tempted to give their money to their kids to 'protect it.' Such a gift can result in a long period of ineligibility for Medicaid benefits and can accidentally generate significant capital gains tax consequences." Gifting should be done only with the counsel of an estate planning attorney who is also an elder law attorney, such as Judy.

It is very difficult to qualify for in-home care from Medicaid. For this reason, and to insure against depletion of your parent's estate, they may wish to consider buying long term care insurance; however, such policies are costly. To get around this, your parents could buy a policy with a limit of a four year payout period, a safe protection limit as the average stay is about twenty-three months for those over age seventy-five. Only one in ten stay in over six years. Be sure the policy covers expenses at home, has an inflation protection, has a thirty-day elimination period for lower rates, covers all levels of care including custodial care, is guaranteed renewable, covers Alzheimer's and any organically-based mental conditions, and covers care in any state-licensed skilled facility.

Also ask about how long the waiting period is for preexisting conditions, waiver of premium, and the company's rating. Look for A+ rated superior companies and agents that have good reputations in the community and with the Department of Insurance.

Another option to consider is a single-premium life policy combined with a long-term care rider. This is a good alternative to the long-term care policy because it creates estate enhancement and gives your parents more money for nursing care than they would have otherwise. A $50,000 CD might purchase $150,000 worth of life insurance. That means three times as much for nursing home care, if it's needed, and three times as much for the heirs if it's not. You should discuss these options with your parents before they become ineligible for insurance coverage due to health problems or advanced age. A good financial planner can help your parents with these decisions.

A reverse mortgage, which allows a retiree to tap into his home equity for living expenses, might be the ticket if your folks need more money. These mortgages are becoming widely available through government and private plans. When your parents take out a reverse mortgage, they use their home as collateral and the lender advances them the proceeds in regular monthly installments. The money is paid back when they sell their home or after their death. Other advantages to reverse mortgages are that your parents can use the funds any way they want and the payments don't affect their Social Security or Medicare benefits. If they receive supplemental security income, reverse-mortgage payments don't affect those benefits, provided they are spent in the same month received. Also, reverse mortgages are available to people who can't qualify for loans based on income or credit history.

The idea may sound great, but reverse mortgages are very expensive. Your parents should have their financial planner or accountant run the numbers for them to see if they wouldn't get a better return by selling their home, buying a smaller one, and investing the balance in an annuity.

Also, ask your parents what they think about life-prolonging hospital procedures. To protect against extraordinary measures to keep your parents alive, the power of attorney agreement must give you charge over the person's health care.

Finally, explain to your parents that you need to know where they keep their important papers. Asking where they are may appear nosy, but your parents will more than likely be glad that someone they trust has this information. Fill out the Parents, Friends, and Advisors sheet below so you can be of help to them when needed.

PARENTS' FRIENDS AND ADVISORS		
	Name	Phone Number
Neighbor/s		
Closest Friend/s		
Doctors		
Emergency Facility		
Attorney		
Accountant		
Financial Advisor		

Now, older clients can go to legal professionals who take a holistic approach to law, advising them about age discrimination, estate planning, probate, guardianship, conservatorship, housing and nursing home issues, Medicare, Medicaid, public benefits, and much more. They are called elder law attorneys and they are usually tied into a network of social workers, psychologists and other elder care professionals to whom they can direct their clients if the need arises.

Help for the Caregiver

Jeff Trowbridge called some of the above professionals when he felt perplexed about his eighty-six-year-old mother, Muriel. She had been calling from Indiana at all hours of the night. Jeff worried continuously about her, but his job as a television production manager in Culver City, California, made it impossible to visit his mother frequently.

"I wanted someone to look in on my mother for safety and friendship," said Jeff. A social worker visits Muriel once a month and remains on call for emergencies. Through a local volunteer group, the social worker arranged for a visitor to drop by Muriel's place once a week to socialize and see if she can do anything for Muriel.

There is a new breed of social workers and nurses who are called geriatric professionals. They coordinate elder care when family members can't. Whether you live in the same town as your parent or across the country, you can hire a geriatric care manager, who is sometimes called a case manager. They will evaluate your parent's physical and emotional condition and determine what care or tests are needed. The care manager can also refer you to doctors, lawyers, accountants, and housekeepers, and also give you information on free or low-cost community resources, such as Meals on Wheels, shopping assistance, and other services.

Care management is a fast-growing and largely unregulated profession. Be especially vigilant about checking references and reputations. Also, check their familiarity with social services and medical facilities in your parents' area. One way to determine whether the agency you are considering is a good one is to find out whether it is certified by Medicare. You can receive a publication titled *How to Choose a Home Care Agency*

by sending a stamped, self-addressed envelope to the National
Association for Home Care, 519 C Street, NE, Washington,
D.C. 20002.

The American Red Cross is another institution that offers
help with your aging parent, as well as your parents' state local
office for the aging, their community's family service bureau,
religious organizations, and neighborhood senior citizen centers. For the specific rules on Medicare call 800-234-5772 for a
free copy of *The Medicare Handbook*. When you call this
number you can ask them for the toll-free number of the
Medicare carrier in your state where you can request a free
copy of the Medicare Participating Physician/Supplier
Directory.

As a Result of This Chapter

What specific issues from this chapter will you want to act on or
keep reference notes on?

19

What Costs Your Kin Money

Happiness is having a large, loving, caring, close-knit family in another city.

—George Burns

Dear Married Taxpayers:

Our statisticians figure that the two of you have probably accumulated a combined estate of over $600,000 by now. This letter is to advise you to remind your executors that federal estate tax will be due on everything over $600,000, payable nine months after the death of whichever of you lives the longest.

Of course, tax is optional for married couples as long as they don't leave more than $1.2 million. If you favor keeping the money in the family, please make the necessary arrangements.

Cordially,
The Commissioner of the Internal Revenue Service

Combat the Fiscal Slaughter of Your Estate

You can disinherit the IRS altogether if your combined estates are no more than $1.2 million if you make the necessary arrangements, that is, set up bypass trusts. You'll want to discuss your estate tax outlook with an estate attorney. Meanwhile, here's the bare minimum you need to understand to make your choices:

Exemptions: Every individual, married or single, is entitled to pass along as much as $600,000 to her beneficiaries before prompting federal estate or gift tax. In theory, you and your spouse should be able to transfer a tax-free total of $1.2 million.

Marital deduction: A married person can leave any amount to her spouse without immediate tax. In effect, tax on these marital deduction assets is simply deferred until the later death of the spouse, unless the assets are consumed.

Simple wills: "Dear Judge: Now that I am dead, these are my instructions as to how I want my property distributed." That is all a simple will is: Your instructions, documented correctly, as to how you want your property distributed. It is the judge's duty to read your instructions and see that they are carried out.

The pitfalls of the simple will: A will does not avoid probate. Does this matter to you? Maybe. The cost of probate is estimated to be 4 to 10 percent of the gross value of the estate. For example, on a property worth $150,000, the probate fees would be approximately $9,000. This is based on the full $150,000, even if there is a $100,000 mortgage on the property. The cost of probate varies from state to state.

Another problem is described in the following example: The husband has $600,000, and the wife has $300,000. He dies first, and his simple will leaves everything to her outright. That means his entire $600,000 qualifies for the marital deduction. At the wife's death, the IRS comes in and picks up $114,000 in the form of federal estate tax. Why? Because she leaves a total of $900,000 to the heirs, and her estate will not be allowed to claim her husband's $600,000 exemption as well as her own. The chance to use his exemption was forfeited when his simple will qualified his $600,000 for the marital deduction.

Here is a better way: By leaving his $600,000 in living trust with bypass provisions for his wife's life benefit, the husband can achieve these objectives without wasting his exemption. Typically, she would receive all the income from the trust as long as she lives. At her death the trust fund would be divided as its terms direct.

To create a living trust, you deed your house, and other major assets such as your automobile, from yourself to yourself as trustee. You are the initial trustee and the initial beneficiary of the living trust. As long as you are alive, you continue to manage these assets just as before. When you die, the alternate trustee takes over and distributes your property as you specified in the trust. Deeding your assets into your living trust will not cause a property tax reassessment.

A living trust has another very important feature. If you should become unable to make financial decisions, your alternate trustee, such as your spouse or adult child, takes over management of your assets in the living trust. This avoids having a conservator appointed.

To summarize, the major benefits of a living trust are avoidance of probate costs and delays, as well as management of your assets if you should become unable to do so. The disadvantage is the nuisance of having to transfer title of your assets to your trust.

Foil Uncle Mooch's Raid on Your Estate

Intestate succession means you left no will or trust thereby allowing the state in which you resided to determine how your estate is to be distributed. In some states as much as two-thirds of your estate could go to your minor children, leaving your spouse with little support. Plus, in certain cases, all sorts of other long-lost relatives could claim rights to your estate. Tom Styskal, estate attorney with the law firm of Kinley and Styskal in Tustin, California, told workshop participants, "It never ceases to amaze me how many families have Uncle Moochs whom no one ever knew until the demise of a relative."

Many of my clients have told me, "I don't know where to begin, and besides I wouldn't understand the lingo." If mass confusion is causing you to procrastinate, an excellent book to read is *Plan Your Estate* by Denis Clifford (Nolo Press, Berkeley). Another helpful idea is to have a financial planner or the trust department of a bank help you through the process of determining what you want stated in your will, the advantages and disadvantages of bypass trusts, and understanding the language of your attorney. I have often sat down with my clients and gone over paragraph by paragraph exactly what the client interprets to be in these documents, listing any questions and concerns to go over with their attorneys. The trust department or financial planner could match you up with the attorney best suited to your needs and personality.

As a Result of This Chapter

What one thing caught your attention from this chapter?
    What has changed for you?

V

What Makes You Money

20

Safety and Other Myths

Opportunity is missed by most people because it's dressed in overalls and looks like work.

—Thomas Edison

When was the last time you were immobilized by the fear that you would make the wrong decision? Can you define or recall the source of that fear? If your family crest becomes the Cringing Chicken at the thought of investing, perhaps you had an experience like ecological engineer Mark Harrison had as a child.

His Uncle Bud made an investment in which he lost his money. Mark heard how horrible it was. The angry words of his father play over and over in Mark's mind: "What a disaster! Why, your uncle should have known better. Your aunt saves and saves, and your uncle goes and blows it all on something and somebody he know nothing about."

Today, Mark's subconscious recalls the emotions expressed during that experience, and his fears are fanned like the flames in the updraft of a forest fire. His attitude leans toward feelings of loss, which subsequently arouses feelings of dread.

In the above tale, Mark aspires for high returns on his savings, but at the same time his fear persuades him to keep his money safe in the bank. Rather than take the time to understand financial concepts, he leaves his money in the safe, guaranteed accounts. In the long term, the only thing "guaranteed" about these accounts is the loss of Mark's purchasing power. Why? Because of the impact inflation has on your lifestyle.

The object of this chapter is to help you to acquire an understanding about the effects of inflation on your future, and to learn strategies to take advantage of inflation.

Get Out of Your Own Way

Attitude, when aviators use the word, refers to the direction an airplane is leaning. When your attitude leans toward feelings of fear, your objective reasoning becomes overwhelmed, and you are unable to take steps that are to your benefit.

What would happen if you changed your internal attitude about investing? What would happen if new information could be used effectively to bridge your value differences and free you from your fears? What if you were given very small, logical steps that would give you an objective understanding of how to invest?

If your aspiration is to gain a higher return, change your internal attitude about investing by taking it upon yourself to accept the challenge of learning about investments. Shift your viewpoint by keeping an open mind as you peruse this section and undertake the workouts. Think of this section as a challenge. Challenges are fun. They turn obstacles into opportunities. You can learn to turn inflation into your opportunity.

Just the Facts, Ma'am

in-fla-tion *n*. 1. An inflating or being inflated. 2. An increase in the currency in circulation or a marked expansion of credit, resulting in a fall in currency value and a sharp rise in prices."—*Webster's New World Dictionary of the American Language*

Inflation has been right around 5 percent annually for the last several years. Or, you can think of it another way: The fall in currency value has been more or less 5 percent annually for the last several years. Generally, financial folks have been using this figure of 5 percent as an assumption of future inflation. There are those that predict mass depressions and extreme changes in lifestyles that will alter that percentage dramatically. But for every one of those, you can find fifty opposing opinions. We could be much more technical about specific inflation numbers, but you are reading this book because you want to eliminate the technical stuff and get rolling.

Why do we have inflation? Simply put, because of the Employment Act of 1946. This was supposed to be the cure-all for our economy by stabilizing prices and promoting full employment. Congress's idea was that brilliant government administrators would foster high employment rates by carefully stimulating inflation. So what has actually happened since this act was passed? The dollar held its own in only two years, and inflation went from an average of 2 percent in the 1950s to an intermittent high of 19 percent in the early 1980s, and back to an average 5 percent since the mid-80s; and according to the U.S. Department of Labor's Consumer Price Index, the purchasing power of the U. S. dollar has had a 59 percent loss since 1976.

Same Dollar, Less Security

Question: What backlash does inflation at 5 percent have on your future lifestyle?

To illustrate what a tremendous difference an investment that keeps up with or even outpaces inflation versus a "guaranteed" investment has on your money, let's look at a hypothetical account of two brothers who are now in their eighth decade, Jack and Hubert Trekker. Back in January of 1976, each of them invested $200,000. Hubert wanted to keep his money where he was guaranteed not to lose a dime of his principal, so he locked it up in certificates of deposit. Over the past fifteen years, with an average interest rate of 8 percent, Hubert received $240,000 in interest. Hubert thought he was safe and set for life with an income of $16,000 a year. At that time, it was quite possible to live comfortably on $16,000 a year along with his Social Security income. However, at an average of 5 percent inflation per year since 1976, in 1990, Hubert needs more than $31,000 in income to buy the same goods and services he bought in 1976 for $16,000.

Jack had a different goal. Jack wanted an investment that would protect his "purchasing power"—his ability to buy tomorrow what he is able to buy today. How Jack's $200,000 nest egg will fare in the years to come remains to be seen. But this is how he did by investing $200,000 in the Standard & Poor's 500 Composite Index fifteen years ago, reinvesting all the dividends and then withdrawing 8 percent of his account each year. Since that time, Jack has received $360,802 in income while his original $200,000 more than doubled to $468,600 by the end of 1990. In 1990, Jack's income from his account was $42,177 while Hubert's was still $16,000. In some years the amounts of Jack's withdrawals would have declined, but overall they would have grown at a much faster rate than the cost of living.

Granted, the latest fifteen-year period had performed significantly above average in terms of investment results. So, how would Jack have made out over an average period?

Taking every fifteen-year span over the past fifty years (and there are thirty-six of them), you'd find that the median was the stretch between 1958 and 1972. Over this period, Jack would have collected $340,970 and his account would have grown to $309,425.

Jack recognized that a rising income is the best hedge against rising prices. He understood that over the long haul, an investment in stocks, and the income that they produce, would continue to grow, reflecting the growing earnings and dividends of the companies in which the S & P 500 invested.

Year	Amount Withdrawn	Account Balance
1976	$ 16,000	$231,619
1977	18,530	196,443
1978	15,715	193,539
1979	15,483	213,760
1980	17,101	266,016
1981	21,281	231,752
1982	18,540	263,045
1983	21,044	301,078
1984	24,086	295,717
1985	23,657	365,635
1986	29,251	404,452
1987	32,356	393,175
1988	31,454	426,583
1989	34,127	527,212
1990	42,177	468,600
Totals	**$360,802**	**$468,600**

Flight of the Cringing Chicken

If your skin still becomes clammy and your mind trips off into a trance at the thought of the word "investing," it is very important to identify and clarify your feelings and thinking. Your goal here is to become an objective judge about investing. The following workout is designed to help you spot your negative thoughts and fears. On a legal pad:

- List three negative emotions that creep into your mind

when you consider putting your money into equity investments rather than in the bank
- Explain or recall the source of those feelings
- Consider whether or not you foster a fear of failure and if you believe failure to be so painful that you won't even try
- Estimate how the effects of inflation influence your future financial safety
- Consider how much procrastination is involved if you are not following through with an investment plan
- Weigh how much better your life would be today if you had started your program five years ago
- Reflect on what the ultimate price is that you will pay if you don't take the first step toward developing your investment plan
- Imagine having achieved your goals and experience the gratification and the good feelings of self accomplishment
- List five objectives you visualize reaching by improving your rate of return

Are you afraid to invest because you fear you will lose what you have?

To aid you in objective thinking, and to expedite your commitment to improving your rate of return, the following chapter introduces you to time strategies, diversification principles, dollar-cost averaging, and the pros and cons of being a passive investor (a good place to start) or an active investor.

As a Result of This Chapter

What long-term (more than five years) commitment did you think of while reading this chapter?

Is this goal important enough to you to become more knowledgeable about how to position your money to work harder for you?

21

Shifting to Investment Thinking

If you don't like what you're doing, you can always pick up your needle and move to another groove.

—Timothy Leary

When I am stuck in L.A. traffic, and the radio plays the lottery jingle, daydreams of what I would do with that much money whirl through my mind: Five-year travel extravaganzas, a villa in Puerto Vallarta, and hideaways in Bermuda and Aspen. The five times I have bought a lottery ticket, I tried to improve my odds by making deals with the powers that be. "If I win the lottery, one-third goes to charity." I even upped the ante to two-thirds to charity and named the charity. Five times someone else made a better deal. Nothing personal, I tell myself.

In any case, whether you are a winner of such games or you are still waiting for your number to come in, learning how to profit on the money you accumulate is the quickest way to double it and still get a good night's sleep.

The Double-Your-Money Formula

The first thing investors always want to know is, "How fast can I double my money?" In fact, you have been scanning this section trying to find out how to double your money. Okay, let's get this question handled. The answer depends on how active and aggressive you are with your money. The more aggressive you are, the more risk you take.

To figure out how long it will take you to double your money, use the Rule of 72. The following workout takes you through the process:

Divide 72 by the rate of return.

Example: Passbook savings account rates are, historically, 5 percent.

72 divided by 5 = 14 years + about 4 months.

If you want your money doubled sooner, let's talk about a 12 percent yield instead of 5 percent.

Example: A return on an investment is 12 percent.

72 divided by 12 = 6 years.

Alternatively, dividing 72 by the number of years in which you want your money to double gives an estimate of the interest rate required.

Obviously where you invest your money makes a difference. With the Rule of 72, you can see that at 6 percent, $10,000 becomes $20,000 in twelve years and at 12 percent, $10,000 becomes $20,000 in six years. In twelve years at 12 percent, the $10,000 becomes $40,000.

Because of individual values, some people thrive on an aggressive approach, while, for others, a conservative approach is all they can tolerate. Furthermore, the words "aggressive" and "conservative" have different definitions to different people. What you want to learn is how to invest with the time you have. Is it worth the stretch to learn how to get a better return and ascertain how much risk you can tolerate? You bet it is.

Two Investment Strategies to Grasp

Start by understanding the following two strategies clearly:

1. Should you become a lender or owner when you invest?
2. Do you want to be an active investor or an inactive investor?

Lender or Owner: Pigeonhole your belongings (assets is our word for it) under the following two categories:

1. Loaned assets
2. Owned assets.

Loaned assets are investments secured by IOUs backed by assets or other features such as government guarantees. These assets position you as a lender, which is what you become when you put money in your savings account and receive interest. The interest you receive is the money the bank pays you for using your money. What you have here is a guarantee of your principal (your initial investment) at maturity (some future date), and a guarantee as to rate of return, but you do not take part in the future value of the investments nor any increase in the profits of the bank. Some of these investments are:

Money market accounts offered by banks or money market mutual funds invested in short-term IOUs. These accounts have replaced the old savings accounts because investors have become aware of their higher interest rates. Money markets offered by banks tend to pay slightly lower yields than the funds because the banks are required to keep a certain amount on deposit in the Federal Reserve Bank in order to guarantee the account up to $100,000. The rates change daily along with changes in short-term interest rates.

Certificates of Deposit (CDs) are IOUs issued by banks affirming that you have given them a certain amount of money for a set amount of time at a specific rate of interest. CDs are insured up to $100,000 by the U.S. government.

Bonds, which are the IOUs of government or corporations, are issued to finance expansion or pay debt. Unlike CDs, bond values go up and down daily due to changes in interest rates. You want to know what assets or other features secure the bond.

Owned assets are investments from which you share in the profits generated by your investment, such as the income produced from your investment. You also benefit from any increase in value of your property, which is known as your capital gain. You do not have a guarantee of principal, nor a guarantee as to your rate of return, but you do take part in the future value of your investment. You participate in any profits or losses from these investments. Some of these assets are:

Stocks, which give you a part ownership position in a company. You can make money two ways: from dividends (income produced by the company) and through capital gains (increase in the value of your stock).

Real estate, most commonly your home.

Any collectibles (stamps, coins, comic books) that you own.

Active or Inactive Investing: Investment vehicles (another word for assets) are classified as either passive or active. You invest in passive investments when you don't feel like taking much time with your investments. These vehicles include money market accounts or funds, CDs, bonds backed by the United States government, and mutual funds, because after you have selected the ones that fit your criteria, the management responsibility is up to the manager of the fund.

On the other hand, active investments, such as individual stocks, corporate bonds, real estate, precious metals, and collectibles require that you gain knowledge of these investments and spend time following and managing them.

The Investment Difference

Think of investing like skiing. If an experienced skier swishes down a steep and precipitous mountain, you assume that he will make it. You enjoy the thrill of watching his professional abilities. On the other hand, you hold your breath and hope a beginner makes it down the same slope alive. But if the beginner masters certain techniques, he can avoid injuries. The same goes for investing.

To understand when to be a lender or owner, and to change the word "gambling" into the word "investing," here are three tactics to follow:

1. Time strategies
2. Diversification
3. Dollar-cost-averaging

Time Strategies

If you are going to need your money in less than five years, use the "loaned assets" approach and find the highest interest rates you can get from money market mutual funds, money market accounts, CDs, and government backed bonds (Treasury bills and notes). Why? Because your principal is relatively safe and you can withdraw it easily.

For money that you are sure you can leave invested for at least five years or more, mutual funds in stocks are a good place to start because you are looking for growth. When you are interested in spending more time and taking more risk, move into active investments.

Question: Why five years or more? The average length of an up-and-down cycle in the stock market is about five years. The longer you leave your money invested, the more likely it will have time to rebound in the event of a downturn.

Question: Why start with mutual funds? Here's your chance to own stocks in fifty to seventy-five companies. To make life even simpler, the selection and timing of when to buy and sell these stocks is done by a person who lives, sleeps, and breathes the business.

Diversification

The stock market crash of October 1987, the savings and loan institutions' debacle, and the insurance industry crisis may make you want to run for the hills. Diversification of your investment dollars along with appropriate time strategies are your best tactics to protect you.

How much should you be putting where? Obviously, there is no one scenario. In the following workout a few questions and examples will give you a good guideline to get you started and address some of your concerns.

Start by establishing the answers to the following four basic financial ambitions for accumulating wealth:

Emergencies—Have you put away enough money in a money market account to pay for three to six months of your expenses?

Various Family Purposes (bigger house, new car, second home)—Have you bought your home? If not, apply your money toward the down payment of a house or condominium. Real estate prices are not expected to rise as fast as in the past and in some areas they are even depressed, so you may be able to get a better house now than a few years ago. Also, remember, you get a tax deduction for your mortgage interest payments and property taxes. When you plan to buy a house or invest in property, *The Real Estate Book* by Robert L. Nessen explains just about everything you need to know.

If you move a lot, you should evaluate renting and investing the money you would have used for a down payment. With real estate prices slowing or even flat, the commissions, closing costs, and loan points could take money out of your pocket.

A General Opportunity Fund (college education, long term plans for an extended vacation, your own business)—If you have young children, investing for their college education should be paramount in your mind. Growth mutual funds will give you your best returns without your having to be actively involved.

Goals and Needs for Financial Independence—Invest in Individual Retirement Accounts (IRAs), even if it's not deductible. If you are married and both of you work, you can each have your own account. A stock mutual fund is a good investment for these accounts. Additionally, find out if you are eligible to take advantage of a company pension plan or the 401(k) plan at work.

   Look at the goals and time frames that you have established
from previous workouts. If you have goals that require money
within the next five years, then you want to shop around for the
best rates and put your money in the more passive investment
vehicles such as Certificates of Deposits. But if your goals are
beyond five years, look to growth stock funds that have a good
track record.

Dollar-Cost Averaging

It never fails. Every time you plunge into the market, you find
yourself buying in at the top. Then, stocks crumple and you get
so discouraged that you sell, precisely at the wrong time.

   If this is your belief, there's help for you in a profitable
investment strategy called dollar-cost averaging. You can avoid
costly fumbles by investing a set amount of money each month,
regardless of whether the market is heading up or down. With
dollar-cost averaging, you get to pat yourself on the back
whenever you invest. If the market goes up, you can say, "Great,
I just made some profit." If the market goes down, your dollars
can buy more shares than the month before, and you will be in
an even better position for the next time the market goes up. It
is also a satisfying way to invest because once you set up the
system it becomes a way of life.

   Just like paying off your bills, make a commitment each month
to send $100 to mutual fund XYZ (fictitious name). Here's how it
works: The month you start your strategy, XYZ is trading at $10
dollars a share; therefore, that's ten shares you buy. The second
month XYZ drops by 50 percent to $5 a share. You don't like that
but you stick with your strategy and you purchase twenty shares
with your $100. In the third month, the fund has rebounded to
$7.50. Your $100 buys thirteen and a third shares. You now own a
total of forty-three and a third shares worth $325. Since your
investment was $300 for three months, you are already ahead $25
even though the stock is less than your first month's investment.
Think of it as investing on the installment plan.

A Good Time to Invest

An oft-heard question is, "When is a good time to start investing in the stock market or stock mutual funds?"

If you're worried about getting into the market at the wrong time, the following hypothetical story about Freddie the Flop will be of interest to you. Freddie the Flop canceled his dental plan the day before his root canal flared up, his vacation in the Sahara was rained out, and he misses trains but catches colds. There's one thing you can say about Freddie's timing: It's always awful.

So it's no surprise that when he decided in 1974 to invest $5,000 a year in a particular growth fund, he managed to pick the worst possible time. Every year for the past fifteen years he has invested on the very day that the stock market peaked. Let's take a look at how Freddie the Flop has done.

He got $296,000, which means his money has grown at an average compound rate of 16.18 percent a year. See for yourself.

If, perchance, Freddie had managed to pick the best day each year, which was when the stock market was at its lowest, to make his annual investment, his account would now be worth $378,572.

The significant aspect of this story is that even though his timing was terrible, he still fared much better than if he had done what many people are doing today: waiting for the "perfect" time to invest.

Fortunate Freddie.

Your Investments and Your Time

This chapter has equipped you with three skills for investing by introducing you to the concepts of: time strategies for how long you can keep your money invested in what type of investments; time frames when it comes to how much time you want to spend managing your investment portfolio and, therefore, what types of investments (active or inactive) you choose; and dollar-cost averaging to free you up from guessing which way the market is headed.

Date of Market High	Cumulative Investment	Value of Account 12/31
03/13/74	$ 5,000	$ 3,413
07/15/75	10,000	8,870
09/21/76	15,000	15,403
01/03/77	20,000	24,102
09/08/78	25,000	34,610
10/05/79	30,000	55,612
11/20/80	35,000	82,475
04/27/81	40,000	87,349
12/27/82	45,000	114,298
11/29/83	50,000	149,754
01/06/84	55,000	145,871
12/16/85	60,000	190,160
12/02/86	65,000	225,602
08/25/87	70,000	245,934
10/21/88	75,000	296,229

As a Result of This Chapter

What risks do you recall taking in your life that have given you a great deal of excitement and happiness?

22

Courting the Mutual Funds

Don't wait for your ship to come in; swim out to it.
—Anonymous

In the winter of 1891, Dr. James Naismith, an instructor in the YMCA Training College (now Springfield College) at Springfield, Massachusetts, concocted the game of basketball. He stuck a couple of peach baskets overhead on the walls at opposite ends of the gymnasium and organized teams to play his new game. The purpose was to toss a soccer ball into one basket and prevent the opponents from tossing the ball into the other basket. Today basketball is a worldwide sport; and when the National Basketball Association (NBA) has its Eastern and Western Conference playoffs, the nation witnesses athletic professionalism at its height.

Question: What does the origin of basketball have to do with mutual funds? Absolutely nothing unless, of course, you are likening a mutual fund to a sports activity, in this case basketball.

Look at it this way: A basketball team has a group of players, a coach, a reputation, and spectators who come and go depending on the reputation enjoyed by the team. A mutual fund has a group of players (securities which are stocks, bonds, or other kinds of investments), a coach (manager or managers), a reputation (performance ratings), and spectators (shareholders) who come and go depending on the ratings enjoyed by the mutual fund.

Like an NBA team, mutual funds are directed by professional managers who have also earned their position by exceptional performance within the stock and bond markets.

The basketball coach is responsible for coordinating the strengths of the players and developing the game strategies. The coach takes the players in and out of the game depending upon how they are performing. The coach calls time outs and takes the team off the court to give new directions or to interrupt the other team's momentum.

Depending on how each security is performing, the manager of a mutual fund can play or take out of play the securities which make up the mutual fund. The manager can call a time out by selling off a large part of the securities in the fund, putting the money in what is known as a cash position. This is usually done to protect the fund from the momentum of adverse conditions.

If the team and the coach have a good shot at becoming national champions, their reputation grows, and the spectators buy tickets in droves to support the winning team.

Mutual funds are no different. If a mutual fund starts to be known as a winner, investors flock to buy shares and become shareholders of the winning fund.

I'll Buy That

How do you make money from mutual funds? You can earn money in the following three ways:

1. Income: Money earned by the fund is called a "dividend." For most funds, you may take the money you've earned in cash or reinvest it in additional shares of the fund.

2. Capital gains distributions: The profit the fund receives when it sells a security. These profits are paid to shareholders as

a capital gains distribution. Again, you may accept this nice windfall in cash or you may reinvest it in additional shares of the fund.

3. Share price (gain or loss): The increase or decrease in the share price of the fund from the time the shares were purchased to when the shares are sold.

Know Your Mutual Fund's Personality

Mutual funds are like people. They come in all sizes, shapes, and personalities. And like your friends, some mutual funds seem to fit just right and be going in your same direction. However, with mutual funds, that direction is set by your goals and the determination of the level of risk with which you can live without becoming frantic with worry if the market turns down.

When trying to establish which fund is for you, use the following workout to ask yourself:

- How soon do I need to sell my shares?
- Can I leave the money invested for five years or more?
- Can I sleep nights owning shares in a fund that might lose a year's gain in a week? If not, you should stay away from the riskier fund categories. Keep in mind, though, that in the long run the riskier funds tend to pay higher total returns. The tradeoff is that the riskier the fund, the more opportunity there is for intervals of miserable performance.

- What are my investment goals? Am I looking for growth from owning shares in companies, or income from lending money to companies or the government?

To help you with the decision as to which mutual fund is for you, the following list summarizes what each type of fund does with your money.

RISK AND NEED SCENARIO

Your Investment Objective	Type of Funds to Use
If your investment attitude is a true grit approach where volatile market swings don't make you crazy, purchase these funds. They invest in stocks of up-and-coming companies, new companies, troubled firms, and single industries.	Aggressive Growth Small Company Growth Maximum Capital Gains Sector
When you're looking for good appreciation in five years or more and relish the milder market swings that occur with more established companies select a growth fund.	Growth Stocks
When companies grow, they need all the money they earn to fuel their growth. But when companies are more settled, they are able to pay dividends; therefore, funds investing in these companies would provide dividends, but would experience less growth.	Growth and Income
A more conservative approach to the Growth and Income funds is one that invests in a portfolio mix of bonds, preferred stocks, and common stocks.	Balanced
You need income and you are not concerned with growth.	Equity Income Corporate Bond Government Bond Money Market

(Continued)

RISK AND NEED SCENARIO

Your Investment Objective	Type of Funds to Use
You have checked your tax bracket in chapter 8 and you need tax-free income. Tax-free funds buy up municipal bonds, which invest in highways, libraries, marinas, and such. Some bonds are free of state as well as federal tax.	Municipal Bond Tax-Free Money Market
Theoretically these funds own the same stocks as in the Standard and Poor's 500 or other index. The growth, therefore, is the same as that of the index.	Index
You believe a global economy is emerging, and you want to be included in the action. These funds may aim for growth, income, or total return. International funds invest all of their money in foreign securities. Global funds invest both in the United States and abroad. Remember, a weakening dollar boosts the returns of these funds.	International Global
Your intent is to avoid investments in corporations involving the military, tobacco, and liquor industries, or environmentally hazardous companies or those which have poor records in hiring minorities.	Socially Conscious

This May Come as a Surprise to You

You can use mutual funds in your IRA, your life insurance, your annuities, 401(k) and 403(b) plans, and any other version of a pension plan you may have the opportunity to take advantage of. As a matter of fact, since all these vehicles are there for your retirement, growth mutual funds are an excellent investment. Many people overlook this opportunity because of their lack of understanding of how investments work. More often than not they believe that bond funds, particularly U.S. Government bond funds, are the safest way to go. Look at what David Silver, retired head of the Investment Company Institute (the funds' largest trade and lobbying group), told senior reporter of *Money* magazine, Prashanta Misra: "There is a common misperception that investing in a fund that buys triple-A-rated bonds will protect you against losses. Investors must realize that as interest rates rise, share prices fall at even top-quality long-term bond funds."

Investing Decoded

Where do you buy mutual funds? Mutual funds are sold directly by investment companies and financial institutions that manage them or through securities brokers (stockbrokers and financial planners). To buy shares in a fund, call the company or broker and ask for a prospectus. They are required to send you one before taking your money. Study the prospectus to make sure you want to spend your money on the investments and strategies described.

What are the costs? If you're buying what is known as a load fund, a commission will be subtracted by the fund manager to pay the stockbroker or financial planner who sold it to you. Usually, the charge is from 3 percent to 5.75 percent, depending on the fund. There's generally no charge when you sell. However, some load funds do charge an exit fee when you sell, but nothing when you buy. A few get you at both ends, and one or two charge if you reinvest.

On the other hand, if you are buying a no-load fund you won't be charged a commission, but remember, all funds have operating expenses and fees, some higher, some lower.

Why would you buy a load fund? For two reasons: One, you don't want to do your homework and would rather pay someone else to decide which is the best fund for you. If your time is worth more than the commission you would pay a broker, then the "load" in a fund is not an issue. The second reason is you have done your homework, and you are convinced that a particular load fund is for you.

Where do I find easy-to-understand information about mutual fund companies and the funds they sell? To do your homework, there are several magazines such as *Business Week*, *Fortune*, and *Forbes* which track the best-performing funds annually. Tracking your funds any closer than annually will make you crazy. One of the best guides is the annual *Forbes* magazine report in the September issue. *Forbes* rates funds on the basis of performance in both rising and falling markets. The funds are rated for consistency in relation to other funds in both up and down periods. There are rating services that are on the Worldwide Web that will give you a great deal of information as well.

Eight Simple Rules to Follow When Choosing a Fund

1. Don't go for complicated strategies. Forget the hedging, option writing, and other sophisticated gimmicks. Mutual funds don't need them, and they run the operating costs up.

2. Don't overlook the operating costs of a fund. Typically, they hover around 1 percent with international and precious metals funds having a higher "expense ratio" (technical lingo for operating costs); bond funds are slightly less.

3. Make sure that if a fund has solid rates of return that the manager who created them is still there. You are not buying past performance; you're buying a manager's expertise. However, this past year several mutual fund companies have dropped the

one manager/star approach and have decided that a group of managers is the better way to go. I've always preferred the group-manager approach because if one leaves it won't impact the fund.

4. Don't complicate your life with market timing gurus or sector fund switching concepts. They only complicate your life and, furthermore, that's what you're paying the management of the mutual fund you bought to do for you.

5. When you are buying equity funds, be sure to include a global fund in your portfolio. Global funds add to diversification by investing in various industries all over the world, a good play for your portfolio.

6. Be sure the fund has a good long-term track record, one that has performed well over the past fifteen years.

7. Use dollar-cost averaging to protect against down swings in the market.

8. Sell your shares if your fund consistently lags behind similar funds or if, when you reach your financial goal, and set up new goals, you determine that the fund serves no purpose under your new criteria.

As a Result of This Chapter

What action will you take today to develop your portfolio to launch you on your course to financial independence?

23

But It's My Hobby

Make Your Decisions With Your Heart, and What You'll End
Up With Is Heart Disease.

—Chapter heading from Harvey MacKay's
Swimming With the Sharks

You are probably wondering about individual stocks and bonds, real estate, and collectibles, the investments that involve you in a more active role. You invest in any of the above for only one of two reasons: you're willing to spend an inordinate amount of time following the values and projections for the future marketability of your investment, or you're doing it just for fun. This includes option trading, buying and selling pork bellies, comic books, real estate, baseball cards, stamps, coins, precious metals, and diamonds. You get the point.

These investments can be very good to people with the aptitude, sagacity, information, wits, tenacity, and patience to handle market fluctuations, and who have an eye for value. However, this book was designed to help you focus on various aspects of your financial life about which you have been indecisive because you just didn't know quite where to start. You were looking for solutions that would cause the least hassle. That is why there has been an emphasis on mutual funds over other investments. On the other hand, you may have a desire to get into a few stocks or maybe you have started a small collection of comic books and wonder if you can make a buck from it. Of course you can.

If you think you would like to start focusing on a particular type of investment, besides acquiring books and going to workshops on the ins and outs of your particular interest, you need to set up a game plan.

The Stock and Bond Business

Generally, stay away from individual stocks until you have about $250,000 to invest, then you can have a well-diversified port-folio, like your own personal mutual fund. That way when a stock takes a nose dive on you, it will only have a small position in a very large portfolio, and you will only take a small loss, which could possibly be offset by the gain of some other stock.

Okay, Aunt Tillie left you $15,000 in her will, and you don't care if you have debit balances on your credit cards; you've always wanted to take a shot at the stock and bond markets. You need to find a broker. Start by interviewing several you have heard about through recommendations from friends, your accountant, and attorney.

Three Questions to Ask a Broker

1. What is your investment strategy?

2. Do you have one particular strategy or do you develop strategies according to the needs of your clients?

3. What sort of a return can I expect from your investment suggestions?

If the broker has one particular strategy on which she focuses, have her go over the pitfalls thoroughly so you know if you can sleep with the consequences. If the broker develops strategies according to the needs of each client, ask where she gets her investment ideas.

After you have gotten to know the broker and think her strategy is for you, here are three questions you will want to ask yourself:

1. Do you feel you can say no to this person when your confidence is waning about a particular stock or strategy?

2. How long has this person been a broker?

3. What will it cost you in fees and commissions? Do you have this in writing?

Draw a line down the middle of a legal pad. Write the answers to these questions down on the left side and any negative experiences or feelings you had with each broker you interviewed to help you select the one with which you're the most comfortable.

Caution: Be aware of the broker who is always calling you to buy and sell your stocks or bonds. Excessive trading eats your money up in two ways: through commissions charged when they are bought and sold, and through taxes on your capital gains. The combination could eat up whatever profit you might have made.

Tip: If you want to make your own stock decisions, either through research or throwing darts at a list of stocks, you don't need the services of a full service broker. You can save 30 to 80 percent on your commissions by using a discount broker. Each one has a little different twist to attract your business, so review several of them before you sign up.

For good technical information with regard to brokers, read Jay J. Pack's book entitled *How to Talk to a Broker.* For a book on stocks and bonds, one by Charles Rolo entitled *Gaining on the Market* is an outstanding guide.

Collectibles

An interest in collectibles should always come from love. Buy what you admire and believe you will enjoy. If later the value should decline, or if you decide to sell part of your collection and keep a particular item, you want to be left with something you love.

Collecting for investment purposes is an entirely different strategy than collecting for an exhilarating hobby, a treasure hunt, or just for the sake of collecting. If it is your intention to collect for investment's sake, decide on one category or art form. Go to the library and read everything you can about the subject in which you are interested. Talk to the pros in that field. Find out what economic conditions cause a rise and fall in the prices.

Random collecting tends to be less valuable over the years as individual pieces have less marketability than a cohesive collection. Also, you must keep your collection in mint condition or it loses its value. In other words, you can't allow your child to play with those magnificent porcelain dolls.

Collections are not mutual funds in that they cannot be readily sold in any market. In a down market or in a period of tight money, you could be left wanting desperately for a buyer. The 1991 recession would be a good example of a time when people were not spending so readily. So be sure to set aside a limited dollar amount for your collection and make it only part of your investment portfolio.

Be aware that collectibles do not have a regulating arm such as the SEC (Securities and Exchange Commission) to watch for deliberate dilution of the market by fast-buck artists who find collectibles a good market in which to employ their fast-talking abilities.

Three Tips for Collectors

1. Before you start moving into collectibles, ask around as if you were the seller of the item in which you are considering investing.

2. Be sure to buy in your price range. You don't want to mortgage the farm for an art piece someone has told you is the last of its kind in existence and have the market for it disappear the next day.

3. Buy the best you can afford. Purchase your collectibles from a dealer who will guarantee your purchase price back in the future if you trade in for a higher quality. Additionally, the authenticity of a collectible should be guaranteed against a full cash refund.

With collectibles, prices are cyclical and are highly influenced by the public's perception of what future inflation rates will be. It is important to become knowledgeable about this area so that you can properly hedge your position against future eventualities. In a similar respect, a rising stock market can result in extra discretionary income for investors and create a frenzy of buying collectibles, raising the prices, only to have them collapse when the stock market drops or becomes stagnant. Collectibles are an investment you hold for the long term so you can weather the ups and downs of markets.

One other very important point to be wary of is the possibility of a certain collectible becoming highly diluted, such as the beautiful matching double strand of large, perfect pearls of one Mrs. Morton Plant. In 1916, Mrs. Plant desperately wanted this particular strand of pearls that had been shipped from Paris to Cartier's New York store. Even though such a strand was quite a rarity in 1916, at $1.2 million dollars, Mrs. Plant could not persuade her husband to indulge her. So, Mrs. Plant offered to trade her Fifth Avenue mansion for the pearl necklace and Cartier accepted. But by the late 1920s, Mr. Mikimoto of Japan had perfected a process for creating cultured pearls, and the value of Mrs. Plant's pearls plummeted to $385,000 by 1957. Cartier's mansion, which is their famed landmark building, is now worth $20 million.

What About Real Estate?

Talk-show host and actress Oprah Winfrey said, "Luck is a matter of preparation meeting opportunity." So while you are saving for a down payment toward that first real estate opportunity, prepare yourself with the information. You will need to evaluate if the value of a property you are interested in is bound to increase. Remember, real estate is not a way to get rich quick, even if those hucksters on television are making you feel stupid because you're not wheeling and dealing with them.

Direct Ownership

If you thrive on finding tenants, fixing toilets and roofs, unclogging drains and gutters, mowing lawns, and repairing the damage caused by a small pet, the direct ownership of real estate could be just the hobby for you. In that case, a good way to save for the down payment is to invest in mutual funds for several years. When you have built up a good size portfolio, use part of it for the down payment. As long as you have a good size portfolio, you can make it through the hard times of this very non-liquid investment. The basic concept of real estate ownership is to make a down payment, charge enough rent to cover the debt load, utilities, and upkeep, and take the writeoff on your taxes.

Five to ten years later, instead of selling it for a profit, you exchange it for what the IRS calls "like property" to avoid the capital gains taxes. And on and on goes the cycle until you meet your demise, at which time your kid inherits your properties, sells them, pays the taxes and goes and lives in Europe for five years to have a meaningful experience. Or you can collect properties, pay them off, hire an excellent property manager to find the tenants, fix the roofs, and gather the rents, while you sail around the world on your yacht for the rest of your life.

General Partnerships

If you feel there is money to be made by getting into real estate now, and you don't have enough money to buy a property or you would like to use the money you have to buy more than one property, you can form a general partnership with another person or persons. Be aware that in a general partnership, each partner is equal and each shares equally in the right to conduct business. In other words, one partner can commit the entire partnership to an obligation or debt or purchase. All general partners are equally liable for the business activities of any one partner.

Limited Partnerships

If you don't want all the hassle of direct ownership, but still believe there is money to be made in real estate and you want additional diversification in your portfolio, you can buy a RELP (real estate limited partnership) or a REIT (real estate investment trust).

In a real estate limited partnership, there is at least one general partner who manages the business and retains personal liability for the activities of the business which includes the selection of the properties and their management. The limited partners have no say in running the business; on the other hand, they have no personal liability for any of the actions of the partnership. The liability of the limited partners is limited to the money they invest. This form of investing in real estate is very non-liquid as well.

Limited partnerships have fallen out of favor with investors in recent years because in the early eighties they were overused and abused because of their tax advantages. A great majority of these partnerships were created for tax benefits and could not stand on their own economics when the Tax Reform Act of 1986 placed major restrictions on the use of losses from limited partnerships. When the investors could no longer offset their ordinary income, such as wages, the frenzy buying of these partnerships ceased which affected all the limited partnerships, even those with good economic viability.

Another setback to RELPs were the projections of many general partners that the partnership could be sold in seven to ten years if certain assumptions were met, which seemed plausible in those days of the roaring real estate market. Today, in the doldrums of the market, many investors want out and because of this, there are many, many limited partnership units available today on what is known as the secondary market. Many of these are economically sound partnerships. The attractive ingredient about buying these units on the secondary market is that they have been around for a while, and therefore, are seasoned. Because of this, you know exactly what properties are in the partnerships (not necessarily so when they were originally offered); the history of the management of these properties (that is, how well the general partner has been performing); the economic condition of the region from which the properties come (which can help you determine the future growth of the properties); and the loan to value on the property (that is, how much money has been borrowed on the properties). For your pension plans or IRA, the partnerships that have no loans are the most conservative. Besides, you don't need the tax deductions leveraged properties would produce. Never consider a package that is leveraged more than 30 percent if the cash flow has stemmed from ongoing operations. Ask specifically about this point because there have been partnerships that were designed with various convoluted terms such as reserves created from the limited partners' original investment to keep up an apparent cash flow. Also ask about the lease arrangements: How long the leases have left, how well the tenants have performed, and who the tenants are; and, if there are properties in the partnership that are lagging, you then can determine if this is only a temporary situation which can be turned around by improvements on the property or new improvements in the economic conditions of their regions, or if they are in depressed and overbuilt areas.

If you are interested in such units, be sure to look at several different packages from several different general partners. This is a buyer's market and it will be for the next two or three years, so use this to your advantage and take your time deciding which one is best for you. For more information on this form of

VI

The Years Beyond 2011

24

Looking Forward to Margaritaville

*Where is Margaritaville? When you get there, you will
know it.*
                —Jimmy Buffett, *Tales from Margaritaville*

"I feel I live from quarterly tax payment to quarterly tax
payment. I just think I am finally saving some money to have a
little flexibility in my life and another quarterly tax payment
takes it away," moaned retired marketing executive Mervyn
Hackley, who has a far different outlook than the one George
Burns held to the very end of his life. "I think it's silly. What do
you do when you retire? Play with your cuticles?" Burns said.

Being retired, Mervyn finds little in the way of shelter for his
income. And the alternative minimum tax limits how much
income he is allowed from tax-free investments.

The Financial Cost of Retirement

If you accept the assumption of living longer, healthier lives,
which is why you have been getting out of bed at 4:30 in the
morning to run fifteen miles in the snow and sleet of winter and
the heat and steam of summer all these years, you'll want to be
aware of the impact your longer life will have on your finances
when you are retired. Note the following:

Generally, when you retire your income becomes fixed. Once you leave your career there are no more pay raises, bonuses, or new perks.

On the very day you retire, inflation begins eating away at the assets you have so carefully accumulated. If something costs $40 today, at a 5 percent inflation rate, in ten years it will cost you $65, and in twenty-five years it will cost you $135. If you retire at age sixty-five, at age ninety you'll need $135,000 for the same lifestyle you enjoyed twenty-five years earlier on $40,000. As a health-aware boomer, sitting in a rocking chair to while your days away most likely isn't your idea of living.

Recessions have a tremendous impact on one's income. Because retired people are out of the earnings mode, they become frightened when they see their income slashed as interest rates drop. Psychologically, people feeling fear lose their spontaneity, creativity, and become limited in their thinking. Because of their retirement mentality, instead of digging their way out, they give up and resign themselves to a more limited lifestyle.

The rising cost of health care has a tremendous impact on one's lifestyle. For your generation, a new accounting rule that forces companies to show health-benefit obligations to future retirees as a liability on their balance sheets has companies busily scaling back coverage. Benefits experts say if you're a couple in your mid-forties, you should start preparing for $7,000 to $15,000 in health-insurance premiums and uncovered medical costs for every year you are retired between ages fifty-five and sixty-four and $4,000 to $10,000 per year after Medicare kicks in.

Unlike your parents, you may not be able to count on extensive home price appreciation to help with your retirement goal. If you are fortunate enough to own a home, eventually you will have to sell it to a generation with fewer members than your own.

Robert A. Sirico, in an article in *Forbes* magazine, May 20, 1996, states that many young adults doubt they will receive a dime from Social Security. Sirico goes on to tell us that, "Demographics bear them out. By the first decade of the next millennium, taxes won't keep up with benefit demands."

At first flush this statement may appear exaggerated, but your benefits will be reduced via taxes tied to income levels. Furthermore, Congress has already started to chisel away at the age at which you can collect full Social Security benefits. For people born between 1943 and 1954 you will not be entitled to your full benefits until age sixty-six, and for people born after 1959, the age is sixty-seven. Stay tuned for more adjustments soon.

The Idea of Retirement

For most of America, the long-term goal has been to retire, and to retire as early as possible. However, research tells us that there are three key reasons why people have yearned for an early retirement. Keep in mind that these three reasons came from generations past, motivated by an age when our nation was an industrial society and jobs were redundant and more physically demanding. These three reasons were and are:

- People were tired of doing what they do and saw no other worthwhile alternatives because they expected to have only one career during their lifetime.
- People felt age discrimination would be a barrier to reentering the workforce.
- People were limited by work schedules that dictated that you work full-time, or you don't work at all.

This yearning for retirement holds true today more for those whose job descriptions fall in the above categories and for those whose skills are no longer appropriate for tomorrow's needs, than for those who enjoy creative work. In reality, opinion polls have shown us that most older people don't want to stop working altogether; most want to blend leisure with work opportunities on more flexible terms.

Few people come to grips with the question of whether to disengage from their careers or not until they have reached retirement age or are involuntarily retired. If they choose or have to work, waiting until the last few years before their retirement leaves them in a far less flexible position to start a new career or find the perfect part-time position.

Energize Your Retirement

The good news is you have the time to look at this information with pragmatic vision. Today, rather than having a goal of retirement, alter your thinking to reflect a new goal of financial independence. With today's realities in mind, not the restrictions of an antiquated time, you will have the opportunity to become more than you have ever been.

Because medical science experts are expecting more breakthroughs in the next ten years than they have had since the practice of medicine began, your generation can look forward to a longer, healthier life, both mentally and physically. Thanks to medical science you have a good chance of living well into your nineties, possibly several years past your one one-hundredth birthday.

Look forward to a financial independence you design, one that protects you from inflation, helps you with your taxes and offers you the opportunity to do what you love to do on your terms.

The following chapter introduces you to fresh ideas and innovative concepts for your future.

As a Result of This Chapter

What particular message of this chapter was important to you?

What specific thought occurred to you as you read this chapter?

25

Underwriting Financial Independence

One has not only an ability to perceive the world, but an ability to alter one's perception of it; more simply, one can change things by the manner in which one looks at them.
—from *Even Cowgirls Get the Blues,* by Tom Robbins

Warren Buffett, who is the chairman of Berkshire Hathaway and whose portfolio includes significant ownership in several companies, one of which is Furniture Mart, was asked how he felt about the fact that Rose Blumkin, the chairman of Furniture Mart, had turned 94. Said Buffett, "She is clearly gathering speed and may well reach her full potential in another 5 or 10 years. Therefore, I've persuaded the board to scrap our mandatory retirement-at-one hundred policy."

The good news for your generation is that the workplace has already started to adopt a more flexible work attitude. Consider these changes that would have been unthinkable in generations past:

- Midlife career changes, as well as regular departures from, and reentries into, the workplace have become more commonplace.

151

- Retraining by corporations has become more frequent and now goes beyond learning how to do the same job better. Some firms not only train their employees for new positions and careers, but also teach them how to deal with life changes.
- There are a number of government and nonprofit programs that offer retraining to lower-income level workers and, in a few instances, to every income level.

Retraining enables one to start fresh, to respond to new challenges, and to design a secure future. This arrangement permits a company to use the abilities and connections of its former employees on a more flexible basis, at competitive, market-rate prices, while allowing the employees to be their own masters.

On Your Own

You may want to launch a business on your own that incorporates aspects of your lifestyle and could give you legitimate tax writeoffs. If this is your goal, start before retirement so it will have an established foothold by the time you retire.

If your dream is to do nothing but play golf through your later years, why not represent a line of golf equipment which allows you to play while you work? Or, how about a newsletter about golf facilities around the world? Your golf game becomes your business and many of your expenses could make you money as writeoffs against your taxes. Also, self-employed persons can now deduct 25 percent of the cost of health insurance for themselves and their dependents.

If you operate your hobby as a business, your expenses are deductible and any losses you incur can be used to offset other income. You must have the intention of making a profit. An activity is presumed to be carried on for profit if it makes a profit in at least three of the last five tax years (two out of the last seven years for activities that involve primarily breeding, training, showing, or racing horses).

Investment Ambitions and Commitments

In the fall of 1993, *Forbes* compiled a list of America's richest people. Of the sixty-nine individuals, Warren Buffett headed the list with a net worth of $8.3 billion. He was the only one who obtained his wealth from the stock market, having started in 1956 with $100. Robert Hagstrom, in his book *The Warren Buffet Way*, tells us, "Over the past four decades, Buffett has experienced double-digit interest rates, high inflation, and stock market crashes." Through all the distractions, the buy-and-hold investment strategy is at the core of Buffett's approach.

Warren Buffett is best known in the investment world for his decisions in common stock, but he also buys fixed-income securities for insurance companies owned under the Berkshire umbrella. It is important to understand that fixed-income securities represent a significantly smaller percent of Berkshire's insurance investment portfolio compared to other insurance companies. In 1993, fixed-income securities (cash, bonds, and preferred stocks) represented 17 percent of Berkshire's investment portfolio compared to a typical 60 to 80 percent in most insurance company portfolios.

Designing Your Portfolio for the Millennium

Start today to become knowledgeable about investments. In San Diego, where my practice is, the greater part of my clientele comes from corporations such as Pacific Bell, General Dynamics, AT&T, and others that have been downsizing, right-sizing, re-engineering or whatever term is in for this year. Having to face retirement, voluntarily or involuntarily, is very traumatic. For those who had taken the time to learn about investments, the anxiety of trusting their future to a portfolio of investments is a lot less than for those who did not take the time.

It is my job to help these future retirees understand possible tax pitfalls that could eat up their pensions and the investment options available to them by giving seminars and doing retirement-funding analysis for each one of them personally. The analysis takes them step by step through understanding what type of income they can expect from their investments, given certain assumptions about what type of growth is possible, and how to protect themselves from tax consequences today and in later years.

Today, when designing your portfolio, put the bulk of your money into investments that will help you achieve your most important goal. Since that goal is your future financial independence, you are looking for growth; therefore, stock funds make the most sense. As the amount of money you have accumulated increases, you may want to go into more time-consuming investments such as real estate or collectibles. Below is a chart illustrating the portfolio for a growth-oriented investor.

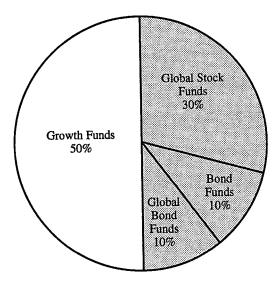

Shifting your attitude toward investing rather than just saving for your financial independence is a pivotal component to your future lifestyle. If you are still squeamish about shifting to investing, start with only 25 percent in a stock mutual fund. Start slowly and learn how to hold for the long term. Increase the percentage, as you gain confidence, to half in stock mutual funds. As your confidence and portfolio size increase, move into international stock funds and stock funds that invest in small and medium capitalized companies. Now, three quarters of your portfolio is in stock funds of various personalities.

For bond funds, look for diversified bond funds that have the opportunity to invest around the world in government and corporate bonds. Be aware that bond funds are not designed to grow and generally are sectored; that is, the fund invests only in a specific type of bond: long-term U. S. Government bonds, short-term bonds, investment grade corporate bonds, and so on. Compare this description with your typical growth fund that invests in seventy-five to five hundred different companies and eleven different industries; industries being utilities, financials, services, technology, and health. When a bond fund that is not diversified is not in favor, your principal investment will most likely go down.

Your goal is to have all but your short-term money invested in various stock funds with an eye to setting up an annual withdrawal of about 8 percent for your later years, your years of financial independence.

As a Result of This Chapter

What specific investment concepts do you feel are important for you to include towards activating your goal of financial independence?

Have you circled dates on your calendar by which you intend to launch your financial independence goals?

Have you circled dates on your calendar by which you intend to accomplish your financial independence?

What are they?

26

Your Portfolio and America's Demographic Shift

Some painters transform the sun into a yellow spot, others transform a yellow spot into the sun.

—Pablo Picasso

When setting up your game plan for investments, trends and demographics should also be evaluated. Since the early fifties, because of the disproportionate size of your generation, the markets have been directed by your needs and decisions.

From Spock to Visa

When you were babies, the baby food industry, which had distributed 270 million jars in 1940, became a leading industry when it ladled out enough strained meals to fill 1.5 billion jars a year by 1953. As you were growing up, a massive pediatric medical establishment arose, and you made Dr. Spock a national figure. When you, were entering school, there were not enough schools for you, and the building industry started to prosper when they filled your needs. When you went to buy your homes, the builders couldn't build them fast enough, so you slept in line overnight to be first for the opening of new housing developments. The building industry continued to grow, and real estate became a prime investment. Since 1986, we have experienced unparalleled continual growth in the stock market, and now in 1996 as you turn fifty, the Masters Tournament of the golf world has taken on a popularity it never expected to experience.

You have lived through the consuming eighties, a decade devoted to the dollar. Through the medium of television, advertisers told you to show the world how powerful you were by the drinks you drank, the labels you wore, the cars you drove, and how many adult toys you owned. Economic gurus encouraged you to buy because inflation would increase the value of whatever you bought then. You were told you deserved to have it all, now. To fulfill this dream, credit cards were made more easily available prompting you to leverage your financial lives as no generation before you ever had.

Since 1980, you have experienced a ride through financial history of various swings in our economy, from runaway inflation in 1980 with money market yields hitting 20 percent, to a runaway stock market in 1987 that crashed on us in October of that year but turned around with a steady growth since then, to money market yields of less then 5 percent in 1991, to the loss of confidence in our savings banks and insurance companies. Through all this, today the boomer generation's values have shifted from the early eighties' go-go highs of spending to the nineties' taking care of basics first.

Advantage: Boomer!

Today your enormous and powerful generation has turned to the belief that less is better through fuel-conserving cars and non-designer clothes, that value for the long term is the priority, and that the constant blitz for consumption is a threat to the environment. You are leading the country toward healthier, more decent lives, and lives that look for what is real, and what

is honorable. Your direction is toward the conservation of
Mother Earth. You have begun to savor, as Europeans and the
Japanese have so long savored, that smaller can be better, that
less can be more if the goods and the services that one buys
deliver real value for one's money. Because of all this, businesses
that deliver quality goods and services will decidedly prosper.
Carefully selecting investments in businesses with these values
will be to your advantage.

You are finding you want to have time to enjoy the laughter of
your children, the indulgence of helping someone in need, the
exploration of your spiritual nature, the tranquillity of a whis-
pering forest and the quiet of the desert, the self-esteem of
rebuilding the infrastructure of your country, and the peace of
mind of financial security. Because of this you are looking for
careers closer to home, with industries that allow you more
personal time. Many of you are converting parts of your homes
into your new place of business. Industries responding to these
trends will also thrive.

All of this is permanently changing the structure of America's
economy, but more importantly, it is the foundation of new
growth in America. Today, you're positioning yourselves to take
over the stabilizing of the economic problems of our country:
the savings and loan crisis, and our personal, corporate, and
international debt, which all weigh heavily upon our financial
system. You are in the mood to introduce and accept any deficit-
reduction program that is both reasonable and equitable so long
as you are convinced that everybody in our society will be
making sacrifices.

Coupled with your leadership are new opportunities that
weren't even available at the beginning of the decade as the
free-enterprise system becomes recognized around the world as
the path to prosperity. Countries once diametrically opposed to
our political and economic system are embarking on new
political structures fashioned after the United States economic
model. Even China is testing opportunities through certain
private industries. This, combined with the plans to unify

Europe, opens great new markets and creates new trading partners for the United States.

Today Is Important

You are where your thoughts and actions during the last few years have brought you. Whatever you will be encountering in your next ten or twenty years will be influenced by what you do today. Wherever you are, it is the place to start. The effort you expend today does make a difference.

Knowing what you expect from life and what you want to contribute to life equips you with the enthusiasm and magnetism to succeed with shrewd and prosperous decisions. The changing world offers new and potentially unlimited economic opportunities for those who are willing to make an investment in your future by learning and taking advantage of these opportunities. Grab hold of your uniqueness as you answer the question, "What new challenges do I visualize?"

As a Result of This Chapter

What antiquated traditions are no longer clouding your mind?

What unique personality traits have you allowed to develop?

What mere outlines of thoughts came to mind as you read the last chapter with your new shift in attitudes?

What specific steps will you take today to develop the answers to the above question toward a more flourishing and valuable lifetime?

What outlandish thing do you want to be doing at age ninety?

Appendix A
Compounded Rate of Return Matrix
(assuming $1,000 initial investment)

YEAR	4.10%	5.00%	6.00%	7.00%	8.00%	9.00%	10.00%	11.00%
1	$1041	$1050	$1060	$1070	$ 1080	$ 1090	$ 1100	$ 1110
2	$1084	$1103	$1124	$1145	$ 1166	$ 1188	$ 1210	$ 1232
3	$1128	$1158	$1191	$1225	$ 1260	$ 1295	$ 1331	$ 1368
4	$1174	$1216	$1262	$1311	$ 1360	$ 1412	$ 1464	$ 1518
5	$1223	$1276	$1338	$1403	$ 1469	$ 1539	$ 1611	$ 1685
6	$1273	$1340	$1419	$1501	$ 1587	$ 1677	$ 1772	$ 1870
7	$1325	$1407	$1504	$1606	$ 1714	$ 1828	$ 1949	$ 2076
8	$1379	$1477	$1594	$1718	$ 1851	$ 1993	$ 2144	$ 2305
9	$1436	$1551	$1689	$1838	$ 1999	$ 2172	$ 2358	$ 2558
10	$1495	$1629	$1791	$1967	$ 2159	$ 2367	$ 2594	$ 2839
11	$1556	$1710	$1898	$2105	$ 2332	$ 2580	$ 2853	$ 3152
12	$1620	$1796	$2012	$2252	$ 2518	$ 2813	$ 3138	$ 3498
13	$1686	$1886	$2133	$2410	$ 2720	$ 3066	$ 3452	$ 3883
14	$1755	$1980	$2261	$2579	$ 2937	$ 3342	$ 3797	$ 4310
15	$1827	$2079	$2397	$2759	$ 3172	$ 3642	$ 4177	$ 4785
16	$1902	$2183	$2540	$2952	$ 3426	$ 3970	$ 4595	$ 5311
17	$1980	$2292	$2693	$3159	$ 3700	$ 4328	$ 5054	$ 5895
18	$2061	$2407	$2854	$3380	$ 3996	$ 4717	$ 5560	$ 6544
19	$2146	$2527	$3026	$3617	$ 4316	$ 5142	$ 6116	$ 7263
20	$2234	$2653	$3207	$3870	$ 4661	$ 5604	$ 6727	$ 8062
21	$2325	$2786	$3400	$4141	$ 5034	$ 6109	$ 7400	$ 8949
22	$2421	$2925	$3604	$4430	$ 5437	$ 6659	$ 8140	$ 9934
23	$2520	$3072	$3820	$4741	$ 5871	$ 7258	$ 8954	$11026
24	$2623	$3225	$4049	$5072	$ 6341	$ 7911	$ 9850	$12239
25	$2731	$3386	$4292	$5427	$ 6848	$ 8623	$10835	$13585
26	$2843	$3556	$4549	$5807	$ 7396	$ 9399	$11918	$15080
27	$2959	$3733	$4822	$6214	$ 7988	$10245	$13110	$16739
28	$3080	$3920	$5112	$6649	$ 8627	$11167	$14421	$18580
29	$3207	$4116	$5418	$7114	$ 9317	$12172	$15863	$20624
30	$3338	$4322	$5743	$7612	$10063	$13268	$17449	$22892

Appendix B

In the Information file put:

- your name/s, address, city, state and zip
- phone numbers (indicate day/evening)
- Social Security numbers
- occupations
- ages as of January 1
- the names, social security numbers, relationships, and ages of dependent children living with you
- names, relationships, number of months with you, gross incomes, and percentage of support by you of other dependents
- any information, forms, or receipts you don't know what to do with, with a note of explanation to your tax advisor

Additionally, answer yes or no to the following questions and include them in the file:

1. Have either you or your spouse become legally blind?

2. Were there any births, adoptions, marriages, or divorces in your immediate family during the year?

3. Are any of your unmarried dependent children nineteen years of age or older?

4. Did you or your spouse receive a distribution from a pension, profit-sharing, or retirement plan? If yes, enter the amount and include tax form 1099R.

5. Did you purchase or sell your personal residence? If so, include escrow and other details.

6. Did you purchase or sell other real estate? If so, include escrow and other details.

7. Did you sell any stocks, bonds, or other property during the year? If yes, include the following information: the description, date acquired, date sold, sale price, and cost.

8. Did you (or your spouse) receive income during the year from any other source not listed under the file headings? If yes, include details.

9. Does anyone owe you money which you have not been able to collect and which has become a bad debt? Include the amount.

10. Did you pay for services for the care of one or more dependents to enable you to work during the year? If yes, include: the number of dependents and the amount paid for dependent care. (The definition of a dependent is one who lives with you, whether a child or step-child, but not a dependent parent.)

11. Did you have an interest in any foreign bank accounts?

12. Did you pay taxes to any foreign country on income being reported this year?

13. Did you make gifts to any one individual of more than $10,000 during the year?

14. Did you make federal and/or state estimated tax payments for the tax year in question? If so, include date paid and amount to the federal government and to the state.

15. Were you audited by the Internal Revenue Service or by your state tax board during the year? If so, include all correspondence.

16. Did you pay rent for a personal residence during the year? If so, include the landlord's name and address.

In the Income file put:

- wages and salaries, including copies of all W-2 forms with the name of your employer(s)
- information on pensions and annuities, include amounts received and all copies of W-2P forms
- partnership, estate, or small business income (include schedule K-1 for each entity)
- installment sales (principal payments received)
- alimony received
- disability income
- state income tax refund
- unemployment compensation

- other income and applicable forms (such as Form 4070 for cash tips of $20 or more) which do not have a special file
- Social Security benefits received (indicate separately, the amounts for husband and wife)

In the Adjustment to Income file put:

- alimony paid, to whom and his or her Social Security number
- forfeited interest penalty on savings withdrawal
- amounts paid into your individual IRA accounts
- indications of whether you or your spouse are qualified participants in an employer plan
- indications of whether you or your spouse are in a self-employed retirement plan and the contribution you and/or your spouse has made
- other adjustments to income
- If you moved thirty-five miles or more in connection with starting work in a new location, include your moving expenses along with:
    the distance from former residence to new job
    the distance from former residence to former job
    expense to move household goods and personal effects
    travel, meals, and lodging for moving self (and family)
    pre-move house-hunting expenses
    temporary living expenses in new area for thirty days
    expenses involved in breaking old lease and/or obtaining new lease
    expenses involved in selling old home and/or buying a new home
    reimbursement not included in W-2

In the Dividends/Capital Gains and Interest Income file:

- list all dividends, including:
    whether it is a joint or separate account (and whose)
    name of payer

       is it taxable or nontaxable
       has there been any backup withholding, and how much
       (include the 1099-DIV forms you receive from the payers)
- list all interest, including:
       whether it is a joint or a separate account (and whose)
       type of obligation (federal, tax-exempt, installment sale,
       insurance policy)
       name of payer
       amount and all applicable 1099 forms (1099-INT, 1099-
       OID)

In the Itemized Deductions file put:

- your medical expenses:
       medical and dental insurance premiums paid
       medicine and drugs
       medical travel
       doctors
       hospitals
       lab fees
       X rays
       glasses and hearing aids
       other medical expenses
- taxes paid:
       state and local income taxes
       real estate taxes
       vehicle license fees
       personal property taxes (licenses for cars, recreational
       vehicles, boats, and mobile homes)
       other taxes
- contributions (remember to include non-cash donations
  such as clothing, furniture, and appliances to thrift shops,
  books to libraries, charitable travel, and any other)
- interest expenses:
       home mortgages paid to financial institutions; first and
       second

      home mortgages paid to individuals; their name and address
- miscellaneous deductions
      union dues
      safety equipment and protective clothing
      small tools and brief cases for work
      required uniforms
      professional dues and subscriptions
      job hunting costs
      education expenses
      other employee expenses
      casualty losses
      other deductions you think may apply
      tax preparation fees
- investment expenses:
      safe deposit box
      investment publications
      investment advisor or financial planner fees

In the Business Income and Expenses file put:

- gross receipts or sales; less returns and allowances
- cost of goods sold
      beginning inventory
      purchases
      cost of labor
      materials and supplies
      other costs
- other income
- business deductions:
      advertising
      bad debts
      bank charges
      car and truck expenses
      commissions
      depletion

    depreciation
    dues and publications
    employee benefit programs
    freight
    insurance
    interest
    legal and accounting
    office supplies
    rent
    repairs
    postage
    supplies
    taxes
    telephone
    travel and entertainment
    utilities
    wages
    other expenses
  • any purchase of business property, including:
    the description
    date acquired
    cost basis
    salvage (what it will be worth when you're done using it)
    life (how soon it will wear out)

In the Rental Income and Expenses file put:
  • gross rental income
  • rental expenses
    interest
    real estate taxes
    insurance
    utilities
    advertising
    telephone
    auto/travel
    cleaning

> garbage and trash
> gardening
> legal and accounting
> licenses
> management fees
> pest control
> supplies
> major improvements
> other

In the Employee Business Expenses file put:

Attention: Signify if this is your "employee business expense" sheet or your spouse's.

- name of employer, address, and occupation
- type of expense, whether it is:
    business/proprietor
    employee expense
    partnership
    miscellaneous
- travel expenses away from home
    fares for airplane, etc.
    meals and lodging
    other
    reimbursement not included in W-2
- car expenses:
    number of months used for business
    total mileage for year
    business mileage for year
    actual car expenses
        lease
        gasoline, oil, lubrication, etc.
        insurance
        repairs, tires, maintenance
        interest, tax, license

      parking

      other

- major purchases of business cars, including

      description

      date acquired

      cost basis (the amount paid for the property)

      salvage

      life

Appendix C

The definition of a "financial planner" has been somewhat elusive, since anyone can put a sign on his door stating that he is a financial planner. You had best sit down and define your needs if you think you want the services of one. *Invest Like Warren Buffett, Live Like Jimmy Buffett* introduces some situations for which you may feel you need financial planning services. But to whom can you turn with confidence?

Do you want someone to help you with your overall financial planning, which would include insurance planning, tax planning, asset planning, financial independence planning, and estate planning? Then you want a Certified Financial Planner (CFP). The CFP designation identifies an individual who has completed the extensive educational, testing, and work experience requirements for the International Board of Standards and Practices for Certified Financial Planners (IBCFP) and has agreed to adhere to the IBCFP Code of Ethics by signing the IBCFP Declaration. Additionally, in order for CFPs to keep this designation, they must continue their education by attending at least thirty hours of classes every two years. Although the CFP designation does not guarantee competence or integrity, it identifies those with the required education and the willingness to subscribe to ethical standards.

Do you just want to buy some insurance? Any licensed insurance salesperson can help you. However, if you want additional expertise, use either a CFP or an insurance salesperson who is a Certified Life Underwriter (CLU). A person with the CLU designation after their name has passed examinations that require a more complete knowledge of insurance than is required simply to sell it.

Do you want someone to help you with your taxes? An accountant will be the person to look for; however, if you have some very complicated tax issues, use a Certified Public Accountant (CPA). As with any of the other designations, CPA after a person's name does not guarantee competence or integrity, but in order for accountants to keep this designation, they must continue their education by attending at least eighty hours of classes every two years.

Do you want someone to help with your estate planning? Although insurance salespeople with the CLU designation, CFPs, and CPAs can identify your estate planning needs and make suggestions, always remember that ultimately, you will need the services of an attorney who specializes in estate planning.

Do you want someone to give you investment advice only, without the other facets of financial planning? A CFP designation is helpful but not compulsory; but if you're paying a fee for advice, your advisor must be a Registered Investment Advisor (RIA). If the person is only selling you investments and is being compensated by commissions only, an RIA is not required, but he must be licensed with the National Association of Securities Dealers (NASD) and this license must be displayed somewhere in his office.

The cost of a financial plan will depend on the type of plan that is being written and the complexity of the case. You'll want to ask your planner up front exactly how he is being compensated for his advice and how comprehensive a plan he is going to develop for you. For example, some planners do not charge fees at all for plans but are paid by the commissions they make from selling the investments and insurance. On the other hand, boilerplate plans are very inexpensive; they run as little as $150 to around $500. For more comprehensive plans, the midrange fees run between $1,500 and $3,500. Some planners charge fees for writing plans that spell out what you need to do on a generic basis, and then charge asset allocation or investment management fees for making specific investment recommendations.

As you can see, there is no standard charge or method of charging. You will have to ask. It is up to you to know exactly what type of information you want from your planner and what type of problems you want solved. If you're uncomfortable with the prices, information, or the gut feelings you have for the person, be sure to take the time to interview other planners until you find one with whom you feel comfortable. One way to know if you would be comfortable with a person is to ask yourself, "Would I be comfortable asking a 'stupid' question of this person or would I feel intimidated by his attitude and pretend the question wasn't important?" Every question is important!

Suggested Reading and Tapes

Age Wave: The Challenges and Opportunities of an Aging America, by Ken Dychtwald, Ph.D. and Joe Flower.

A Whack on the Side of the Head: How You Can Be More Creative, by Roger vonOech.

Creative Thinking (Order tapes through Nightingale-Conant, 1-800-323-5552.), by Mike Vance.

Do It! Let's Get Off Our Buts, by John-Roger & Peter McWilliams.

Generations: The History of America's Future, 1584 to 2069, by William Strauss and Neil Howe.

Life Trends, by Jerry Gerber, Janet Wolff, Walter Klores, and Gene Brown.

Megatrends 2000: Ten New Directions for the 1990s, by John Naisbitt and Patricia Aburdene.

The Popcorn Report: Faith Popcorn on the Future of your Company, Your World, Your Life, by Faith Popcorn.

The Sky's the Limit, by Dr. Wayne Dyer.

Think and Grow Rich (book or tapes), by Napoleon Hill.

Tough Times Never Last but Tough People Do! by Dr. Robert Schuller.

What Color Is Your Parachute? A Practical Manual for Job-Hunters and Career Changes, by Richard Nelson Bolles.

Index